Cambridge Ele

Elements in Politics and Society in Southeast Asia
edited by
Edward Aspinall
Australian National University
Meredith L. Weiss
University at Albany, SUNY

ETHNICITY AND POLITICS IN SOUTHEAST ASIA

Amy H. Liu
University of Texas, Austin

Jacob I. Ricks
Singapore Management University

CAMBRIDGE
UNIVERSITY PRESS

CAMBRIDGE
UNIVERSITY PRESS

University Printing House, Cambridge CB2 8BS, United Kingdom

One Liberty Plaza, 20th Floor, New York, NY 10006, USA

477 Williamstown Road, Port Melbourne, VIC 3207, Australia

314–321, 3rd Floor, Plot 3, Splendor Forum, Jasola District Centre,
New Delhi – 110025, India

103 Penang Road, #05–06/07, Visioncrest Commercial, Singapore 238467

Cambridge University Press is part of the University of Cambridge.

It furthers the University's mission by disseminating knowledge in the pursuit of
education, learning, and research at the highest international levels of excellence.

www.cambridge.org
Information on this title: www.cambridge.org/9781108927796
DOI: 10.1017/9781108933179

First published 2022

A catalogue record for this publication is available from the British Library.

ISBN 978-1-108-92779-6 Paperback
ISSN 2515-2998 (online)
ISSN 2515-298X (print)

Ethnicity and Politics in Southeast Asia

Elements in Politics and Society in Southeast Asia

DOI: 10.1017/9781108933179
First published online: February 2022

Amy H. Liu
University of Texas, Austin

Jacob I. Ricks
Singapore Management University

Author for correspondence: Amy H. Liu, amy.liu@austin.utexas.edu

Abstract: What explains the treatment of ethnic minorities in Southeast Asia? This Element conceptually disaggregates ethnicity into multiple constituent markers – specifically language, religion, and phenotype. By focusing on the interaction between these three ethnic markers, Liu and Ricks explore how overlap between these markers can affect whether a minority integrates within a broader ethnic identity; successfully extracts accommodation as unique group; or engages in a contentious and potentially violent relationship with the hegemon. The argument is tested through six case studies: 1) ethnic Lao in Thailand: integration; (2) ethnic Chinese in Thailand: integration; (3) ethnic Chinese in Malaysia: accommodation; (4) ethnic Malays in Singapore: accommodation; (5) ethnic Malays in Thailand: contention; and (6) ethnic Chinese in Indonesia: contention.

Keywords: ethnic boundaries, ethnic conflict, ethnic integration, ethnicity, identity, minorities, Southeast Asia

ISBNs: 9781108927796 (PB), 9781108933179 (OC)
ISSNs: 2515-2998 (online), 2515-298X (print)

Contents

1 Introduction

Most visitors to *Danau* (Lake) Toba in North Sumatra take time to enjoy a performance of *si gale-gale*, a life-sized wooden marionette whose movements invoke the spirit of the dead at funeral ceremonies. The practice, presented daily for tourists, displays local Batak culture. Indeed, much of the area's draw is the ethnic Batak identity. Utilizing ethnicity for tourism is specific to neither Lake Toba nor Indonesia. Throughout Southeast Asia, the region's thriving travel industry markets ethnicity to the world – from Kayan women's neck rings in Northern Thailand to Balinese Barong dances, from the promotion of tribal tourism in the Philippines to Singapore's sanitized enclaves of Chinatown, Little India, and Kampong Gelam.

Such portrayals, however, present ethnic distinctiveness in a positive light. They neglect the potential tensions, struggles, and accommodations necessary in such an ethnically diverse region. Beyond tourist performances, Southeast Asia is home to simmering ethnic insurgencies and destructive riots – not to mention violent military crackdowns on minorities (see Barter 2020). For instance, in 1998 riots in Indonesian cities targeted the ethnic Chinese, destroying businesses, homes, and churches. Dozens of rapes were reported, and more than 1,100 died – most of them rioters trapped in burning buildings. In another example, the post-2004 conflict in Southern Thailand between the Malay minority and the Thai state has resulted in more than 7,200 deaths. Even more devastating, since 2017 the Myanmar military's efforts to purge the Rohingyas culminated in more than 700,000 refugees and tens of thousands of deaths. Why are some ethnic cleavages the stuff of tourist dreams while others become violent nightmares?

We argue that the propensity for conflict largely depends on the markers defining ethnic boundaries. Ethnic identities are those created through attributes that are transferred – or believed to be transferred – through ancestry or by descent (Chandra 2006: 398). Central to these identities are markers used to stipulate group membership or lineage – for example, appearance or customs. These indicators allow individuals to identify as members of an in-group and to demarcate where their in-group ends and the out-group begins (Barth 1969; Wimmer 2013).

Scholars largely agree that such ethnic boundaries are constructed, whether through institutional factors or the actions of individual leaders (see, e.g., Chandra 2004; Horowitz 1985; Posner 2005; Wimmer 2013). Even so, building a social barrier between groups requires some raw materials – that is, it presupposes the existence of markers. In this Element, we recognize the fabricated nature of ethnicity. And from here, we argue that ethnic boundaries are mutually constituted through the existence of distinctive markers, as well as the behavior of actors who utilize these markers. Specifically, we are interested in markers that are descent-based and have a high degree of visibility: for example, *language*, *religion*, and *phenotype* (Chandra 2006). The distribution of these highly visible markers – what Chandra and Wilkinson (2008) call *ethnic structure* – becomes the building blocks for demarcating group boundaries. We contend that how these markers overlap influences behavior – that is, *ethnic practice* (Chandra and Wilkinson 2008). In other words, ethnic markers are simultaneously the tools available to political actors and the constraints that bind them in their efforts to bridge or buttress ethnic boundaries.

In the pages that follow, we present a theory about the relationship between two ethnic groups who serve as our main actors: the minority and the hegemon. The degree to which ethnic markers overlap between these groups helps determine whether ethnic boundaries are rigid or impermeable – which in turn results in three stylized outcomes. First, if multiple overlapping markers exist, then boundaries become porous and easily crossed, thereby increasing the probability for minority **integration** within a broader identity. In an environment of multiple overlapping markers, both the minority and the hegemon will have sufficient cause to overlook ethnic distinctions in favor of focusing on the shared markers. There is ground for ethnic integration wherein the minority is considered a part of or subset of the hegemon identity. Second, when the two groups share no overlapping markers, the groups are in a space of potential **accommodation**, wherein the minority is more likely to be recognized as a unique group. The impermeability of boundaries means there is no marker for the minority to identify with the hegemon. And the hegemon, who sees no common ground between themselves and the minority, faces a stark choice: They can either engage in costly violent suppression or acknowledge minority distinctiveness. This acknowledgment means managing differences through accommodative policies such as allowing for the use of the minority language in public, institutionally protecting the minority religion, and legally recognizing the minority group and their distinct rights. Third, when there are few (for instance, only one) overlapping markers, the relationship between the minority and the hegemon becomes **contentious**. In this scenario, one group eyes the singular shared marker and believes that integration is possible; the other group, however, focuses on the alternative markers that accentuate their distinctiveness. This incongruence results in heightened mistrust and an increased probability for conflict. Taken together, our theory predicts a curvilinear relationship: the probability of ethnic conflict is lower when we see either multiple overlapping markers or no common overlaps; in contrast, conflict is more likely to happen in the presence of one overlapping marker.

Ethnic boundaries are thus the aggregation of multiple distinctive markers and the actions of both the minority and the hegemon to utilize these markers for ethnic boundary-making. The boundaries defined by these markers – especially the degree to which they are fixed or porous – can then influence the propensity of groups to cohabitate peacefully or continually grapple with one another.

We will further elaborate our argument later, but first we highlight the ethnic diversity found in Southeast Asia. We then provide a review of recent scholarship on ethnic politics in the region, emphasizing the literature's high degree of country-specificity, resulting in (1) attention to one particular dimension of ethnicity; and/or (2) a focus on one particular minority that has been prone to conflict. Missing are a conceptual appreciation for the compound nature of ethnicity, a theoretical framework for understanding how the different markers interact and affect ethnic politics, and an empirical analysis both across countries and across groups. We then detail our theory.

Ethnic Groups in Southeast Asia

Identifying and measuring ethnic groups is no easy feat (Abdelal et al. 2009; Csata, Hlatky, and Liu 2021). Southeast Asia is no exception. **Table 1** lists the major ethnic groups (up to five) for each of the eleven Southeast Asian countries according to four different sources. The numbers in the first column are the official figures per the national government. In nine countries, these numbers are from the census or a census-like government survey. Note that the referenced census is not always the most recent. In some countries (e.g., Vietnam), the most recent census did not include questions about ethnicity. Additionally, there are countries (such as Myanmar) that did ask about ethnicity but have yet to release the data. And finally, there is the likes of Thailand, which does not ask about ethnicity directly, but rather about language and nationality.

The second set of numbers is from the Central Intelligence Agency's *World Factbook.*[1] International organizations (e.g., Minority Rights Group) and crowd-sourced platforms (e.g., Wikipedia) frequently rely on the *Factbook* as an authoritative volume. The sources for the numbers, though, vary and are "what we judge [as] the most reliable and consistent data for any particular category." Note, however, that "[s]pace considerations preclude a listing of these various sources."[2] The third set of numbers is from the *Ethnic Power Relations* dataset. The dataset culls information from country expert surveys. The final set of numbers is from the *Asian Barometer Survey.* If the surveys are

---

[1] CIA, *The World Factbook*, 2020, www.cia.gov/the-world-factbook/ (accessed August 13, 2020).
[2] CIA, "Frequently Asked Questions (FAQs)," *The World Factbook*, 2020, www.cia.gov/the-world-factbook/about/faqs/ (accessed August 13, 2020).

Table 1 Ethnicities of Southeast Asia
(Note: Only top five listed if more than five)

	Official Numbers (Varying Years)	CIA World Factbook (2020)	Ethnic Power Relations (2017)	Asian Barometer (2014–2016)
Brunei	Malay 65.8% Chinese 10.3% Others 23.9% *2019 Finance Min*	Malay 65.7% Chinese 10.3% Others 24%	Bumiputera 57.0% Chinese 10.0% Bumi (Other) 9.0% Non-Bumi 5.0%	
Cambodia	Khmer: 97.1% Vietnamese 0.4% Lao: 0.2% Chinese: 0.1% Thai 0.01% *2013 Inter-Censal*	Khmer 97.6% Cham 1.2% Chinese 0.1% Vietnamese 0.1% Other 0.9%	Khmer 95% Cham/Malay 2.2% Khmer Loeu 1.2% Vietnamese 0.8% Chinese 0.2%	Khmer 97.2% Cham 1.5% Brao 0.3% Kouy 0.3% Phnong 0.3%
Indonesia	Javanese 40.1% Sundanese 15.5% Malay 3.7% Batak 3.6% Madurese 3.0% *2010 Census*	Javanese 40.1% Sundanese 15.5% Malay 3.7% Batak 3.6% Madurese 3%	Javanese 45.0% Sundanese 13.0% Madura 5.0% Minangkabau 3.0% Malay 3.0%	Javanese 39.2% Sundanese 16.7% Malay 4.8% Madurese 3.9% Betawi 2.8%

Country				
Laos	Lao 53.2% Khmu 11.0% Hmong 9.2% Puthai 3.4% Thai 3.1% *2015 Census*	Lao 53.2% Khmu 11% Hmong 9.2% Phouthay 3.4% Tai 3.1%	Lao 55% Lao Thoeng 12% Lao Tai 12% Khmou 11% Hmong 8%	
Malaysia	Bumiputera 67.3% Chinese 24.5% Indian 7.3% Other 0.6% *2010 Statistics Dept*	Bumiputera 62% Chinese 20.6% Indian 6.2% Other 0.9% Non-Citizen 10.3%	Malay 57.7% Chinese 25.4% East Indian 7.2% Dayaks 3% Kadazan 2.9%	Malay 49.9% Chinese 29.7% Indian 6.9% Iban 2.8% Bidayuh 1.4%
Myanmar	Burmese 66.7% Shan 8.2% Karen 6.0% Rakhine 4.4% Mon 2.3% *1983 Census*	Burman 68% Shan 9% Karen 7% Rakhine 4% Chinese 3%	Bamar 68.0% Shan 8.5% Kayin (Karen) 7% Chinese 3.0% Zomis 2.1%	Bamar 72.0% Rakhine 6.0% Kayin 4.4% Chin 2.6% Shan 2.0%
Philippines	Tagalog 28.2% Cebuano 13.1% Ilocano 9.1% Bisaya 7.6% Hiligaynon 7.6% *2000 Census*	Tagalog 24.4% Bisaya 11.4% Cebuano 9.9% Ilocano 8.8% Hiligaynon 8.4%	Christian Lowlanders 85.9% Indigenous 7.5% Moro 5.1% Fil-Chinese 1.5%	Cebuano 27.5% Tagalog 20.3% Ilonggo 12.9% Ilocano 8.3% Waray 7.4%

Table 1 (cont.)

	Official Numbers (Varying Years)	CIA *World Factbook* (2020)	*Ethnic Power Relations* (2017)	*Asian Barometer* (2014–2016)
Singapore	Chinese 74.1% Malay 13.4% Indian 9.2% Other 3.3% *2010 Census*	Chinese 74.3% Malay 13.4% Indian 9% Other 3.2%	Chinese 74.0% Malay 13.0% Indian 9.0% Eurasian, Other 3%	Chinese 75.8% Malay 11.7% Indian 10.9% Other 1.5%
Thailand	Thai Lang 90.7% Thai & Other 6.4% Malay Lang: 2.2% Local Lang:1.5% Burmese 1.3% *2010 Census*	Thai 97.5% Burmese 1.3% Other 1.1% Unspecified <0.1%	Thai 81.5% Chinese 12% Malay Muslim 5% Hill Tribe 1% Shan 0.5%	Thai 97.9% Chinese 1.2% Other: 0.5%
Timor-leste	Tetum prasa 30.6% Mambai 16.6 % Makasae 10.5 % Tetum terik 6.1 % Baikenu 5.9 % *2015 census*	Austronesian Melanesian-papua Chinese minority	East Timorese 100%	

Vietnam

Kinh 86.2%
Tay 1.9%
Thai 1.7%
Muong 1.5%
Khome 1.4%
1999 census

Kinh 85.7%
Tay 1.9%
Thai 1.8%
Muong 1.5%
Khmer 1.5%

Kinh 85%
Tay 1.8%
Thai 1.8%
Muong 1.5%
Khmer 1.4%

Kinh 93.6%
Thai 3.8%
Hmong 0.9%
Day 0.7%
Nung 0.4%

nationally representative, as they are designed to be, then the classifications and proportions of ethnic groups should also theoretically mirror that of the country.[3] We see Selway (2011, 2015) employ this strategy. The categories and weights are theoretically assigned by the *Asian Barometer Survey* team in conjunction with the national team coordinators.

With a few exceptions, we see robustness when it comes to the largest ethnic group – in terms of both identification and proportion. For example, the Khmer in Cambodia are somewhere between 95% to 97.6%. Likewise, the Javanese in Indonesia are about 39.23% to 45%. And the Bamar in Myanmar number between 66.65% to 71.98%. But beyond the largest ethnic group, we see both tremendous consistency and variance across the four measures.

At one extreme is Singapore. The categories are the exact same (Chinese, Malay, Indian, and Other), and the proportions are all within two percentage points *for each group* across the four measures. For example, Indians number 9.2% per the 2010 national census, 9% per the CIA *World Factbook*, 9% per the *Ethnic Power Relations* dataset, and 10.9% per the *Asian Barometer Survey*. The numbers for Laos, Thailand, and Vietnam are also quite robust, particularly for the larger groups.

At the other extreme, there are the likes of the Philippines and Timor-Leste, where there are discrepancies not just in the *who* and the *how many* but in the *which* – that is, which ethnic cleavage is the relevant one. In the Philippines, three of the measures focus on language: for example, Tagalog, Cebuano, and Ilocano. Yet we see no consistency in the proportions across these languages. Consider that the 2000 national census identifies Tagalog as the largest ethnic group (28.2%). Yet, the same group ranks second in the *Asian Barometer Survey*, with only 20.3%. Likewise, Cebuano speakers are 13.1% in the national census (rank: second) and 9.9% in the CIA *World Factbook* – but an astounding 27.5% (and the largest) in the *Asian Barometer Survey*. This discrepancy could be driven in part by how language is being counted: for example, whether the individual is geographically from the area where that language is dominant, or whether the individual speaks that language at home. It could be the product of interethnic marriages wherein people speak multiple languages. It could also reflect the less-than-successful government efforts to standardize Tagalog as Filipino. These differences, however, do not manifest strictly with respect to language. At a larger, macro

---

[3] Per the *Asian Barometer*, its research protocol requires a national probability sample that gives "every citizen . . . an equal chance of being selected to participate in the survey . . . As such, the samples selected for the Asian Barometer surveys represent the totality of the adult, voting-age population in each country surveyed" (*Asian Barometer*, "Survey Methods," www.asianbarometer.org/survey/survey-methods, accessed March 9, 2021).

level, we see discrepancies in terms of which ethnic marker is the relevant one. While three of the measures for the Philippines look at language, the *Ethnic Power Relations* dataset categorizes groups based on phenotype and even religion: Christian Lowlander (85.9%), indigenous (7.5%), Moro (5.1%), and Fil-Chinese (1.5%).

The inconsistency is most extreme for Timor-Leste. First, the 2015 national census identifies fourteen ethnic groups, primarily along a linguistic cleavage – with Tetum Prasa constituting 30.6% of the population. Next, the CIA *World Factbook* focuses on phenotype: Austronesian, Melanesian-Papua, and Chinese minority – with no proportions provided. Third, the *Ethnic Power Relations* database identifies only one group, "East Timorese," at 100% – giving us no sense of the ethnic cleavage. And, finally, the *Asian Barometer Survey* does not even include Timor-Leste.

While we can think of a continuum from Singapore (high consistency across measures) to Timor-Leste (low consistency), there is a pair of countries that is both robust but also low consistency: Brunei and Malaysia. The Philippine and Timor-Leste cases notwithstanding, these are the only two countries where the identified largest ethnic group is not consistent across measures. The inconsistency, however, manifests in the same way: Malay versus *bumiputera* (literally, "son of the soil"). In both countries, all Malay are *bumiputera*, but not all *bumiputera* are Malay. The government created the *bumiputera* classification to make the hegemon appear larger – specifically vis-à-vis the Chinese. We see this most clearly in the Malaysia example. The 2010 Department of Statistics estimates the *bumiputera* population at 67.3%, with the Chinese population at 24.5%. These are comparable numbers to the CIA *World Factbook* (62% and 20.6%). However, the *Ethnic Power Relations* dataset disaggregates the *bumiputera* – and in doing so, the Malays are only 57.7% of the population, while the Chinese remain steady at 25.4%, the Dayaks are 3%, the Kadazans are 2.9%, and the Orang Asli are 0.6%. The *Asian Barometer Survey* likewise splits the *bumiputera* – and thus the Malay population drops to just below 50% of the survey sample. The Iban are 2.8%, the Bidayuh are 1.4%, and the Melanau are 0.3%.

As will we demonstrate, the (in)ability to generate consistency on which ethnic marker manifests (e.g., language or phenotype), the category names (e.g., Malay versus *bumiputera*), and the category proportions across the different measures is testament to the challenge of accurately measuring ethnicity. This is especially important for scholars as measures of ethnicity have a resounding impact on the research they produce (Posner 2004). In this Element, we focus on the politics that shape ethnic categories. However, we also acknowledge that other factors – such as resource constraints, bureaucratic rules, and historical legacies – can create categories that may not necessarily reflect political cleavages (see Hirschman 1986). In the next subsection, we review the recent ethnic politics literature on Southeast Asia.

The Literature

Over the past two decades, scholarship on ethnic politics in Southeast Asia has tended toward fragmentation – often divided by national boundaries and focused on specific countries.[4] Just as the politics of disparate Southeast Asian states take different trajectories, so has the scholarship on ethnicity. And, in most cases, we see specific themes emerging in each country-focused literature.[5]

Consider Indonesia. Much of the recent work focuses on the ethnic-based conflicts that emerged post-Suharto (Aspinall 2009; Bertrand 2004; Chauvel 2005). The *reformasi* era saw rebellions and riots with ethnic undertones throughout the archipelago, with particular attention on three areas due to their separatist foundations: Aceh in the west, Papua in the east, and Timor-Leste. The Aceh rebellion calmed after the 2004 tsunami, and Papua saw a massive military crackdown, with rebels engaging in ongoing violence. Timor-Leste, however, was successful in achieving independence in 1999. Aside from these movements, several local conflicts also erupted throughout the country, with fighting groups often differentiated by ethnicity (Davidson 2008a; Schulze 2017). These instances of violence were particularly devastating in terms of lives lost. Almost 90% of deaths from collective violence between 1990 and 2003 were rooted in ethnicity (Varshney, Tadjoeddin, and Panggabean 2010: 37–40). Explanations for conflicts range from institutions (Bertrand 2004; Tajima 2014) to electoral competition – or the lack thereof (Toha 2017) – to efforts by local communities to reshape power structures post-Suharto (Davidson 2008a; Soedirgo 2020). Since 2004, ethnicity-based violence has decreased rapidly (Aspinall 2011), partly due to electoral institutions designed to reduce ethnic mobilization (Prasad 2016). This has resulted in a new body of work looking at ethnicity's role in electoral politics (Fox 2018) and public goods provision (Tajima, Samphantharak, and Ostwald 2018). Yet, the common denominator across Indonesia-centered research remains the conflict emphasis (e.g., Setijadi 2019; Sumaktoyo 2021).

While the literature on the Philippines is also conflict-dominated, the extent has been relatively limited compared to Indonesia. Despite the islands

---

[4] See Davidson (2008b) for an extensive review of the literature prior to 2005.
[5] Given space constraints, we do not review the ethnic politics literature on Brunei, Cambodia, Laos, Myanmar, Timor-Leste, and Vietnam.

exhibiting multiple potential ethnic cleavages based on language, May (2003) identified the dominant ethnic category of the country as "mainstream Filipinos" – defined by their Christianity and their relatively Westernized behavior. Alternative ethnic groupings are the indigenous mountain communities, the ethnic Chinese, and the Philippine Muslims found mostly in Mindanao. Aside from the Chinese, these groups share a general phenotype and speak Austronesian tongues. A cursory review of the literature finds little research emphasizing distinctions between them, despite eight major language groups and general diversity across the islands. Even the Chinese–Filipino community is well integrated, such that there is little tension between the ethnic Chinese and their counterparts in the "mainstream" group. Thus, the Philippines exhibits relatively few ethnic conflicts. The one major exception is the division between the Christian majority and the Islamic minority in the south (Mendoza 2021). The colonial powers called the Muslims "Moro," thereby amalgamating multiple smaller linguistic groups that shared little commonality beyond their religion. But both Spanish and American colonial management helped unify the groups; moreover, post-independence efforts to centralize state control strengthened the Moro identity (Abinales 2000; Mendoza 2021). The Moro identity today is brandished by the separatist organizations in the region (e.g., the Moro Islamic Liberation Front). The Moro–Philippine conflict has been the central focus in much of the recent ethnic politics research on the Philippines (Kaufman 2011, 2013; Sterkens, Camacho, and Scheepers 2016). Thus, the politically salient ethnic cleavage in the Philippines literature is religion.

Like the work on conflict in the Philippines, scholarship on ethnicity in Thailand has generally focused on the Malay Muslims in the south – a region that has experienced a violence surge since 2004, largely due to state mismanagement. Here, the literature has emphasized the Malay identity based on the historical Patani Sultanate in the area, which was never fully integrated into the Thai national identity (Liow 2009; McCargo 2008, 2012; Selway 2007; Streicher 2020). Put differently, religion is only one aspect of the conflict; a broader cleavage exists, drawing from linguistic differences and historical legacies (Anusorn 2019; Harish 2006), coupled with government efforts to castigate Muslim Thais as less than patriotic (Ukrist 2006). We return to this cleavage later in this Element. The literature on Thailand's ethnic politics, however, is not limited to conflict. There is a growing body of scholarship examining ethnic integration throughout the rest of Thailand (e.g., Ricks 2019; Saowanee 2021; Selway 2020, 2021; Wasana 2019). Per official narratives, many observers consider Thailand as ethnically homogenous. Yet the supposed homogeneity masks substantial diversity; it ignores how the Thai state has systematically erased ethnic cleavages (Streckfuss 2015). Despite this, linguistic, class, and political differences continue to exist in tension with the state-approved national identity (Draper and Selway 2019; Saowanee and McCargo 2014, 2019). Thus, recent work on ethnicity in Thailand is bifurcated between scholars working on conflicts in the south and researchers focusing on integration efforts elsewhere.

In contrast to Thailand's homogenization efforts, Malaysia and Singapore have maintained – if not outright embraced – the communal distinctions imposed during British colonial rule. Ethnic politics research in these two countries has relied on broad ethnic categories: Malay, Chinese, Indian, and Other (in the case of Singapore). The largest tensions that appear most commonly center on Malay–Chinese relations.

In Malaysia, research has focused on communalism, specifically the creation of a Malay identity and Malay nationalism; the exclusion of the Chinese minority; and the tensions that exist between the two groups (see Liu 2015a). Additionally, work on Eastern Malaysia notes the capacity of political parties to mobilize ethnic identities as campaign strategies (Prasad 2016). Indeed, political parties are central to ethnic politics throughout Malaysia. The Barisan Nasional, for example, was an alliance between the ethnically delineated parties of UMNO (Malay), MCA (Chinese), and MIC (Indian) – thus providing the strength for UMNO rule. UMNO's ability to rule, however, weakened as Chinese Malaysians – dissatisfied with the pro-Malay policies – abandoned the MCA (Noh 2014). Nevertheless, ethnic Malays remained largely loyal to UMNO, which allowed the Barisan Nasional alliance to survive until 2018. Even when Malays defected from UMNO's (and Najib Razak's) corrupt image to former Prime Minister Mahathir Mohamad's Malay-nationalist Bersatu party, the new set of political arenas was still defined by ethnic concentrations (Abdullah 2019; Ostwald and Oliver 2020). In short, ethnic parties remain a mainstay of the Malaysian ethnic politics literature.

In Singapore, the Chinese majority is overwhelmingly dominant. Yet, the PAP (People's Action Party) government has striven to both maintain ethnic categories and to minimize their impact. Indeed, the Singapore state has framed itself as multiracial to prevent any ethnic community from becoming the basis for national identity (Chua and Kuo 1998; Liu 2015a). Hence, research on Singapore has focused on the ability of the state to take a diverse society and "engineer" identities to reduce ethnic fragmentation (Barr and Skrbis 2008; Kong and Yeoh 1997; Ostwald 2014; Ostwald, Ong, and Gueorguiev 2019; Tan 2018). The state ascribes all Singaporeans an ethnic identity and then heavily regulates that identity (Stimpfl 2006). With stringent Out-of-Bounds (OB) markers, the government restricts discussions of ethnic and religious divisions, including obvious markers – for example, the hijab – that could serve to differentiate communities (Abdullah 2016). Research on Singapore thus reflects the ability of a determined state to manage its ethnic diversity.

In short, recent studies of Southeast Asian ethnic politics have been dominated by country-specific studies that emphasize one particular ethnic dimension, whether ethnoracial differences, ethnoreligious conflicts, or ethnolinguistic parties. And because of this targeted attention, the focus is often on one singular minority – for example, the Muslims in the Philippines or the Chinese in Malaysia. Such specificity, while providing extensive detail, limits the questions that we can ask. For instance, why have the Chinese in Thailand been able to integrate but not the Chinese in Indonesia? Why has Singapore demonstrated more success than Malaysia at managing diversity? Why does religion become a mobilizing cleavage for some groups but not for others? Such questions require a different level of theoretical abstraction and a comparative research design. In this Element, we contend ethnicity is a compound concept that warrants disaggregation into multiple constituent markers (Chandra 2006); we provide a theoretical framework for understanding how interactions between the different markers can affect ethnic politics (Selway 2011, 2015); and we empirically demonstrate our claim using a most-similar design at both the country and group levels (Slater and Ziblatt 2013). We elucidate this next as we discuss the three markers of interest in our study of Southeast Asian ethnic politics.

Disaggregating the Concept of "Ethnicity" in Southeast Asia

We focus on three specific ethnic markers that can create ethnic boundaries: language, religion, and phenotype. These markers are what Chandra (2004: 37) calls "costless" or highly visible cues (Chandra 2006: 416–417). They are costless in that they can be used for identification without expending effort or resources. For instance, an individual can easily assume the ethnic identity of another based upon their speech, name, dress, or features. Conversely, indicators such as homeland or history require both parties to share information before ethnic identity can be determined. Costless indicators are therefore particularly useful in determining the boundaries between the in-group and out-group, particularly in low-information environments.

Even so, identifying and measuring any one of these three markers is no easy feat because of politics. Take **language,** for example. What is the difference between a language and dialect? From a linguistic perspective, the answer is about mutual intelligibility. When two vernaculars share high overlap – often above 85 percent – they are considered dialects of the same language. And when the overlap is low, they are classified as two different languages (Lewis, Simons, and Fennig 2016; Liu 2015a). However, when governments fail to recognize a vernacular as a distinct language but instead label it as a dialect, they deny speakers of that vernacular their own group identity. In Singapore, for example, while Chinese is an official language, the recognized dialect is Mandarin (also known as "common talk") – despite large Cantonese-, Hakka-, and Hokkien-speaking populations (Liu 2015a). These vernaculars are not only mutually unintelligible with Mandarin, they are also unintelligible with each other. While all four share the same orthography, the same cannot be said for speaking. Mandarin has four tones; conversely, Cantonese has nine; and the lexical similarity between the two is 19 percent (Liu 2021; Tang 2009). This is by no means specific to the Chinese language or the Singapore state. The Thai state vaunts homogeneity, labelling vernaculars with a regional prefix – for example, northeastern Thai – thereby considering them part of the Thai language. Yet, mutual intelligibility between northeastern Thai and central Thai (also known as "standard Thai") is low. In fact, from a linguistic standpoint, northeastern Thai is more akin to Lao than to central Thai (Ricks 2020; Smalley 1994).

The politics of counting language is not just about denying distinct vernaculars their recognition as languages (see Lieberman and Singh 2017). It can also run in the opposite direction: It is the promotion of what is linguistically a "dialect" into a language. In Indonesia, the official language is Indonesian. Yet, from a linguistic standpoint, it is very similar to Malay. To unify the archipelago against the Dutch, there was an effort to create a panethnic identity, and this identity necessitated a distinct language. To this end, the government renamed Malay as Indonesian (Anderson 2006; Liu 2015a).

There is also a challenge with measuring language size. While individuals have mother tongues, this does not mean they cannot learn a second or third language (Liu and Pizzi 2018). In fact, it is possible that they may develop higher proficiency in one of these languages than in their mother tongue. Conversely, the mother tongue can mean either the language spoken at home or the ancestral language. If it means the ancestral language, there is no guarantee that an individual can use the language proficiently. A good example of this is Singapore's Lee Kuan Yew (LKY). Despite being of Chinese heritage, the language he used at home was English. When LKY went to England for schooling, he experienced isolation from the other ethnic Chinese students who spoke Chinese vernaculars. It was not until he returned to Singapore – and later as an adult – that he mastered Chinese (Lee 1998). This anecdote highlights how language can be learned. It also demonstrates how LKY would be seen as Chinese despite his initial shortcomings because – as defined by the postindependence census – it was his ancestral language. Given the politics of identifying languages, it is not surprising that we see substantial variation in which languages – and, correspondingly, which ethnic identities – are recognized in each Southeast Asian country.

The second ethnic marker of interest is **religion**. Like language, religion can be difficult to measure. While different groups may profess fealty to the same deity, there may be variations, whether in doctrine or in intensity. At what point does this variation warrant the two groups being viewed as different religions versus two sects? On the one hand, a larger belief set may lump a minority belief set under an encompassing religion umbrella. On the other hand, it is possible that the larger belief set excludes the smaller one from the religion completely so as to discredit their doctrine. And just as people can learn languages, people can convert into a religion (or abandon it) – thereby suggesting religion is also distinct from religiosity.

Furthermore, not all religions behave alike with regard to fractionalization; the degree of polarization matters. A religious group that perceives itself to be under threat may emphasize its identity more than one that is secure in its hegemony (Montalvo and Reynal-Querol 2002). This fluidity can make this marker difficult to measure. At the same time, however, religious symbols can be easily flaunted. Of particular use are names, dress, and speech patterns. Individuals seeking to identify themselves as pious can adopt clothing and speaking styles that call attention to their religiosity. They may also assume religious names. The challenge, then, is measuring the intensity of divisions within and between faiths.

The third ethnic marker is what we call **phenotype**. Phenotype is about the individual's observable characteristics, where the characteristics are often the result of genetic makeup. Phenotype is also frequently referenced as "color" or "race" (see Horowitz 1985). Both terminologies, however, have heavily western-centric, colonial-derived origins – such as where there was a need to differentiate "scientifically," in a taxonomical fashion, the "white" people from the nonwhites. Certainly, there are genetic differences; but even so, these genetic differences can be subject to politicization. Consider the Chinese in Southeast Asia: From Indonesia to Malaysia, from Brunei to Singapore, the Chinese are seen as phenotypically different. But farther up the mainland – from Vietnam to Thailand to Cambodia – someone can be of Chinese heritage and be ethnically Vietnamese, Thai, or Khmer based upon other criteria, such as language. Thaksin Shinawatra and Hun Sen, for example, are two men that have considerable political influence in their respective countries. They are seen as Thai and Khmer, respectively. Yet at the same time, they both have clear links to their (Teochew) Chinese heritage.

The Chinese are not the only group that is seen as phenotypically different. Indians – or, more broadly, South Asians – are seen as distinct in some countries (e.g., Myanmar). One of the grievances the Papuans (and later the Timorese) had against the Indonesian state from the outset was phenotype: While Indonesians are Austronesians, Papuans are Melanesians (see Chauvel 2005). Again, as with the other ethnic markers, phenotype can be politicized or ignored.

Each of these three markers is salient in Southeast Asia – although the degree of salience varies. In some cases, such as conflicts in Indonesia and parties in Malaysia, ethnicity has a high degree of political salience. Conversely, in other cases, such as in Singapore and in most of Thailand, ethnicity is less salient in the political arena – albeit via different mechanisms. In the next subsection, we turn to a theoretical explanation for why we see variation in the political salience of ethnicity – that is, the treatment of ethnic minorities.

A Theory on Overlapping Markers and the Treatment of Ethnic Minorities

In this Element, we draw on the works of Selway (2011, 2015) and call attention to the relationship between these three ethnic markers. For starters, ethnic markers can – and do, but not always – overlap (i.e., cross-cut). In some instances, ethnic markers can be completely exclusive, meaning the categories for one marker match perfectly with the categories of a second (and third) marker.[6] For illustration purposes, let us imagine a population wherein there are two languages (*Language 1* and *Language 2*), two religions (*Religion 1* and *Religion 2*), and two phenotypes (*Phenotype 1* and *Phenotype 2*). Let us assume everyone in **Group 1** uses *Language 1*, practices *Religion 1*, and is of *Phenotype 1*. Conversely, everyone in **Group 2** uses *Language 2*, practices *Religion 2*, and is of *Phenotype 2*. In this extreme example (see **Table 2**), there is no overlapping marker whatsoever. The two groups have completely exclusive ethnic identities. Thus, if we met someone who uses *Language 1*, we would know their religion and phenotype with certainty. Likewise, if we met someone who practiced *Religion 2*, we would know their respective language and phenotype. In short, ethnic boundaries are apparent and fixed.

Alternatively, ethnic markers can completely overlap. At this other extreme, an imaginary person who uses *Language 1* has a 50–50 probability of practicing *Religion 1* or *Religion 2*. Moreover, for each religion, there is another 50–50 probability of being either *Phenotype 1* or *Phenotype 2*. And the same is true for *Language 2*. Here, we cannot infer the individual's religion or phenotype based

---

[6] Per Selway (2011, 2015), there are no cross-cutting cleavages.

Table 2 Examples of overlapping markers

	No Overlapping Marker			All Markers Overlap	
	Minority	**Hegemon**		**Minority**	**Hegemon**
Language	All use **Language 1**	All use **Language 2**	*Language*	Half use **Language 1** Half use **Language 2**	Half use **Language 1** Half use **Language 2**
Religion	All practice **Religion 1**	All practice **Religion 2**	*Religion*	Half practice **Religion 1** Half practice **Religion 2**	Half practice **Religion 1** Half practice **Religion 2**
Phenotype	All appear **Phenotype 1**	All appear **Phenotype 2**	*Phenotype*	Half appear **Phenotype 1** Half appear **Phenotype 2**	Half appear **Phenotype 1** Half appear **Phenotype 2**

on what language they use. If the population were equally distributed again, the probability of an individual having any mix of these markers is 12.5 percent. Simply put, with extensive overlapping markers, we cannot claim to know an individual's ethnicity based on one identified single marker. Of course, these percentages are only for demonstration purposes; in reality, such equally sized groups are highly unlikely.

The interaction of these three markers, then, determines the perceived porousness of the ethnic boundaries – which in turn shapes the interaction between ethnic groups. For theoretical purposes, we consider two main actors: (1) the *hegemon* – a politically dominant group that typically controls the state and the narrative of which identity types are acceptable; and (2) a minority group. The hegemon prefers total incorporation of all minorities within the hegemon-approved identity; conversely, the minority's preferences are conditioned on what the hegemon offers. If the offer is a flexible arrangement – that is, if integration costs are relatively low – the minority will be willing to integrate. As boundaries become more fixed, and integration costs increase, then the minority is less willing and able to integrate. If the hegemon believes it is offering integration, but the minority refuses the offer, this becomes a possible source of conflict. Alternatively, if the minority believes it is integrating and demands acknowledgment for its efforts, but it falls short of the hegemon's demands, again conflict is likely. However, if both sides perceive integration as impossible due to a lack of overlapping markers, then accommodation is probable, though certainly not guaranteed.

We argue that the degree to which ethnic boundaries are perceived to be permeable or fixed based upon these cross-cutting ethnic markers shapes minority and hegemon decisions. We propose three idealized types of treatment – although these categories can certainly bleed into one another. First, when the minority and the hegemon overlap on multiple markers – that is, when there is only one distinct marker – ethnic boundaries are relatively porous. In this scenario, we should see **integration**: namely, (1) *efforts by the hegemon to consider the minority as part of the hegemon with some qualifications; and (2) the minority largely willing to accept the hegemon's terms.* By analogy, the minority is seen as a half-sibling and should be invited to the proverbial family dinner. The hegemon is able to focus on the shared markers. Likewise, the minority will have incentives to integrate. Joining gives them access to resources that they would not otherwise enjoy. And while the minority can theoretically hold on to the distinct marker, it is more likely that over time this uniqueness will fade into the background. But here, it is important to note that integration rarely happens exclusively because of a carrot. There is usually a stick as well. Put differently, while it may "make sense" for the minority to integrate, this calculation is made against the backdrop of a hegemon-controlled state that can – and sometimes does – exert violence.

Second, when the two groups have no overlap whatsoever on the three markers, we see (almost) impermeable ethnic boundaries. For the minority, in the absence of *one* common denominator, there is no mechanism that allows them to be able to identify with – that is, integrate into – the hegemon. There is no incentive to replace their mother tongue. Likewise, there is no rationale for them to convert. And if phenotype is seen as something exclusive, then that is also hard to change. Given the complete separation, the hegemon has no mechanism – short of outright repression or ethnic cleansing, which does sometimes occur – to force integration. Under such conditions, their second-best option is **accommodation**: *the legal acknowledgment of minority distinctiveness and institutional efforts to manage the differences.* Examples of this management can include teaching the minority language in schools, developing the minority religion in a public space, and recognizing the group as a racial category on the census. Note, however, that just because there is accommodation does not mean the two groups are equal. Ethnic politics is inherently hierarchical. Even when the government extends de jure recognition, it often comes with de facto restrictions.

And finally, when the minority and hegemon overlap on just one of the three markers, we expect a high probability for **contention**: *a relationship characterized by heightened mistrust by one group and (the possibility of) conflict.* There are two ways for contention to unfold. The first is that the hegemon believes the one overlapping marker is sufficient to warrant the minority as a cousin. The hegemon views ethnic boundaries as permeable; there is also an expectation that the minority will "choose" to abandon their ethnicity. Thus, we see integration efforts by the state. These overtures, however, are not always welcomed. From the minority perspective, their attention is not on the shared marker but on the two non-overlapping markers, wherein the group perceives ethnic boundaries to be firm. The distinct identifiers do not make the group some sort of cousin – they outright make them different clans. And when the minority rebukes integration efforts by the state, the hegemon responds – often with repression. And at some point, we see a feedback loop whereby the minority pushes back and mobilizes, electorally if not violently.

Conversely, in the second contention type, it is the minority that believes the one shared marker is sufficient for a dinner invitation. However, the hegemon focuses on the two mismatched markers, and as long as their attention is on the mismatch they will view the minority with skepticism. Overtures by the minority to demonstrate their shared kinship are only seen as threats. The hegemon will respond by demarcating the boundaries between the two groups firmly – even if the boundaries must be moved continuously in response to minority efforts. This demarcation can also result in contention, if not violence.

To summarize, the presence of multiple overlapping markers lowers ethnic barriers – thereby facilitating opportunities for integration. The story is different when ethnic markers do not provide overlap. If both the minority and the hegemon see ethnic boundaries as fixed, there is a possibility for the groups to negotiate accommodation. However, if one group believes the boundaries are fixed but the other attempts integration, we see greater likelihood of conflict. Put differently, the perceptions of impermeability of ethnic boundaries are central to whether the relationship between a minority and the hegemon leads to integration, accommodation, or contention.

Lest this theory appears overly deterministic, we emphasize that we are working with the above-described probabilistic events through ideal types. We can think of our theoretical predictions like a Kuznet's Curve (see **Figure 1**). Conflict likelihood is low when the boundary is highly permeable due to multiple cross-cutting dimensions. Here we expect integration between the minority and the hegemon. As boundaries become more fixed – but where boundaries are considered permeable by only one group – we predict a higher probability for conflict. At the far end of the scale, though, where both the minority and the hegemon consider ethnic boundaries to be completely impermeable, we see a widening of our predictions. If the hegemon can engage in ethnic cleansing or repression, then we may see violence – as noted by the

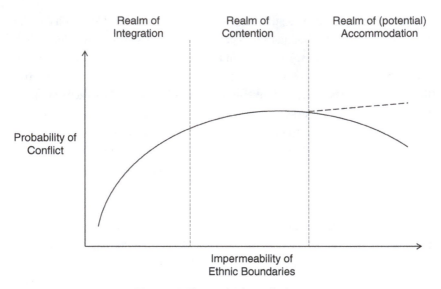

Figure 1 Theoretical predictions

upward-sloping dotted line in Figure 1. If not, then the odds of violence decrease as the groups seek accommodation. In sum, we expect the probability of conflict to be very low when we see multiple overlapping indicators of ethnicity (i.e., permeable ethnic boundaries). The probability of conflict, however, is high when one group (either the minority or the hegemon) sees the boundaries as permeable while the other group sees them as fixed. When both groups consider the boundaries impermeable, then they are more likely to pursue accommodation.

Two related caveats merit discussion. First, how the three ethnic markers overlap between the minority and the hegemon is subject to change. While these are "sticky" markers (i.e., they are difficult to change in the short run; Chandra 2006: 414–416), they can evolve. People can learn new languages, they can convert to different faiths, and people of different phenotypes can intermarry. Such changes can blur the distinctions between groups. Also consider that boundaries are subject to politicization. At one extreme, the state can choose to identify everyone – regardless of diversity – under some panethnic, civic national identity in the face of a large existential threat. And, at the other extreme, even if the identity of a minority evolves to match that of the hegemon, the state can still choose to redraw group boundaries to ensure that the minority will always remain an out-group. In short, boundaries between groups can change over time, especially when politicized.

This discussion about politicization raises a second point. The treatment of minority groups – namely, whether they are integrated, accommodated, or in contention – is in equilibrium. The costs of pursuing a different strategy outweigh those associated with the status quo. But calculations change when there is a critical juncture – that is, a shift in the political landscape. Examples of critical junctures can include transitions from colonialism to independence, from absolute monarchy to limited rule, and from authoritarianism to democracy. Critical junctures are opportunities to reconsider how the ethnic markers match up between the minority and the hegemon (see Bertrand 2004). When there are macro-changes to the political landscape, whether (and to what extent) the hegemon will tolerate ethnic differences may also change. If the hegemon sees an overlapping marker, it may seek to build on that similarity. Whether the minority acquiesces will depend on how many overlapping markers exist, against the backdrop of whether the state can use violence. And when there are no shared markers between the two groups, the state must decide whether to accommodate or fight. Accommodation is less than ideal, but at a critical juncture – such as when there is an external threat – it may not be possible to fight.

Politicization of Ethnic Markers and Critical Junctures: An Illustrative Case

The case of the Chinese in Indonesia (1945–1998) highlights (1) how the three ethnic markers overlap is subject to politicization; and (2) how the treatment of minority groups is in equilibrium until a critical juncture (see **Figure 2**). During Sukarno's administration (1945–1965), there were no shared markers between the Chinese minority and the *pribumi* hegemon. The absence of any overlap coupled with larger structural threats (e.g., fighting for independence) meant that the government nominally accommodated the ethnic Chinese. However, there were no grand overtures to the Chinese. Instead, they were left alone: Chinese language schools and Chinese-medium radio programs remained in operation.

For Sukarno, Chinese support was essential to secure a pan-Indonesian independence. But once the external threat – and the costs of repression – disappears, what we see is the complete minority subjugation at the first possible critical juncture. On September 30, 1965, junior officers in the Indonesian military – affiliated with the Indonesian Communist Party (PKI) – executed six military generals in an attempted coup (Roosa 2006). In response, General Suharto launched a counterattack. With international support, the army purged the PKI. While the state-perpetuated violence targeted the communists, the Chinese were

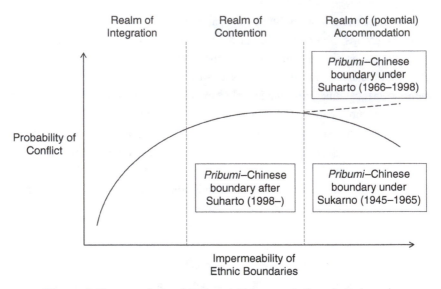

Figure 2 Three periods of *Pribumi*-Chinese relations in Indonesia

inevitably associated with the PKI. Admittedly, much of this violence was opportunistic rather than based on legitimate communist ties (Labini 2001; van der Kroef 1976; Wang 2002; Yahuda 2004). Best estimates are that a few thousand Chinese were killed during this period (Cribb and Coppel 2009). From a relative standpoint, this is a small number considering between 500,000 and more than one million people died during the anticommunist purges. Nevertheless, the Chinese community suffered. It was also during this period that executive power transferred from Sukarno to Suharto – thereby marking the "end of organized political activities of the ethnic Chinese" (Tan 2004: 33). Thereafter, the ethnic Chinese were viewed with suspicion (Suryadinata 1976).

Once in power, Suharto established a series of security agencies. One clandestine body was the State Intelligence Coordinating Body (*Bakin*). *Bakin* was responsible for intelligence assessment and action aimed at the nonmilitary population, namely the ethnic Chinese (Sukma 2003). The belief that the Chinese still had ties with Beijing made the fear of a communist revival a constant threat: there was always the "possibility of subversion and infiltration" (Soeharto 1991: 239). During Suharto's tenure, the government – considering any display as suspicious – banned Chinese culture (Ananta, Arifin, and Bakhtiar 2008): from the public use of the Chinese language to the establishment of Chinese schools, from Chinese mass media to ethnic Chinese organizations, from celebration of Chinese New Year to the use of Chinese-language names (Suryadinata 1976). In contrast to the Chinese in Malaysia who were accommodated (more in Section 3), the Chinese in Indonesia were forcibly integrated (see Suryadinata 2008: 2), despite the absence of shared markers in either case.

As a result of this repression and forcible integration, the ethnic Chinese in Indonesia have largely abandoned their "Chinese-ness" and have "*peranakan-ized*" – that is, they all speak Indonesian (Suryadinata 2008: 5). Put differently, due to the Suharto government's assimilation policies, the Chinese minority have adopted the Indonesian language, thereby making language a new shared marker that would link them with the *pribumi* hegemon. Where the two groups had no overlapping markers, they now share one.

Yet, we will see that this one shared marker is insufficient to prevent conflict. From the perspective of many in the hegemon group, there is an almost impene-trable barrier between the ethnic Chinese and the *pribumi* – a barrier that is episodically reified. It does not help that the ethnic Chinese have been economic-ally advantaged. The class disparity was on full display with the 1997 Asian Financial Crisis. This was a period of heightened violence toward the ethnic Chinese (Wang 2002). With rising inflation and unemployment, the public demanded reforms. Demonstrations – first in Medan – turned violent when protestors began looting ethnic-Chinese–owned shops (Purdey 2006a). The events spread to Jakarta, where mobs attacked the areas around Chinatown in Glodok (Siegel 1998), and then throughout the archipelago (see Purdey 2006b; Wijayanta 1998). The absence of security, coupled with senior government rhetoric (Human Rights Watch 1998), meant many Chinese businesses were burned, Chinese men were violently attacked, and Chinese women were raped. Thousands of ethnic Chinese fled Indonesia (Mulyanto 2019). While the situation has improved since 1998, as we will see in Section 4, the presence of only one shared marker has kept Chinese–*pribumi* relations contentious.

A Most-Similar Research Design

To examine how overlapping markers affect government responses to ethnic differences, we explore ethnic politics in six *group–state* dyads. The first two are the *ethnic Lao* in **Thailand** and the *ethnic Chinese* in **Thailand** – two cases where the minority shares two overlapping ethnic cleavages (religion and phenotype) with the hegemon. In both cases, the outcome of ethnic politics can be characterized as integration. The next two cases are the *ethnic Chinese* in **Malaysia** and the *ethnic Malay* in **Singapore**, where there are no cross-cutting cleavages: there is no shared ethnic marker whatsoever between the minority and the hegemon. The government response in both cases has been a story of accommodation. Finally, the last pair of cases include the *ethnic Malay* in

Thailand and the *ethnic Chinese* in **Indonesia** (1998–). Here, there is only one shared ethnic marker: phenotype in the former, and language in the latter. The result in both cases is contention.

We chose these six cases – these three pairs – because they lend themselves well to a most-similar comparative case design (Slater and Ziblatt 2013). As we see in **Table 3**, all four countries exhibit high levels of ethnic fractionalization. Although Thailand, Malaysia, and Indonesia are indigenously more heterogeneous than Singapore, all four countries experienced religious expansion from West/South Asia, commodity traders from Europe, and movement of laborers from China and India. Moreover, three of the countries share a British colonial legacy: the British colonized both Malaysia and Singapore, and while Thailand technically remained free of a colonial overlord, it was not free of the influence; in fact, it "behaved like [a colony] in many respects" (Tarling 2004: 59). Thailand was forced to accept unequal trade treaties and cede territorial claims to both the British and the French. The state also mimicked the British administrative structure observed in neighboring territories (Wyatt 2003). Because of the "logic of agreement," factors such as demographics, culture, and colonial legacies can be dismissed as necessary conditions.

Additionally, by leveraging six *group–state* dyads – where the same ethnic group appears in multiple states *and* where multiple ethnic groups appear in the same state – we can also eliminate group-specific and country-specific explanations. For example, governments do not respond uniformly to the Chinese minority. In Thailand, the Chinese are integrated; in Malaysia, they are accommodated; and in post-Suharto Indonesia, there is contention. Likewise, as we will see in the Thailand case, the government does not always respond the same way to all minorities: While the state has integrated the Lao and the Chinese to varying degrees, it remains in conflict with the Malay. Finally, these dyads also demonstrate that their outcomes are not the effects of some larger, structural civilization clash. In sum, the variation in outcomes observed across the six *group–state* dyads provides an empirical advantage for testing the theoretical argument.

2 Ethnic Integration

The first outcome we examine is **ethnic integration**: namely, (1) *efforts by the hegemon to consider the minority as part of the hegemon with some qualifications; and* (2) *the minority largely willing to accept the hegemon's terms.* Recall, when a minority shares multiple markers – whether language, religion, and/or phenotype – with the hegemon, ethnic boundaries are relatively porous. The

Table 3 The six cases

	Case 1	Case 2	Case 3	Case 4	Case 5	Case 6
Ethnic Minority	*Ethnic Lao*	*Ethnic Chinese*	*Ethnic Chinese*	*Ethnic Malay*	*Ethnic Malay*	*Ethnic Chinese*
Country	**Thailand**	**Thailand**	**Malaysia**	**Singapore**	**Thailand**	**Indonesia**
	(1893–)	(1900s–)	(1957–)	(1965–)	(1909–)	(1998–)
Cross-Cutting	2 Overlapping	2 Overlapping	0 Overlapping	0 Overlapping	1 Overlapping	1 Overlapping
Ethnic Politics	Integration	Integration	Accommodation	Accommodation	Contention	Contention
Demographics	High Diversity	High Diversity	High Diversity	High Diversity	High Diversity	High Diversity
Colonialism	Quasi-British	Quasi-British	British	British	Quasi-British	Dutch
Nationalism	Ethnic	Ethnic	Ethnic	Civic	Ethnic	Civic
Civilization Dyad	Buddhist–	Sinic–	Sinic–	Islamic–	Islamic–	Sinic–
	Buddhist	Buddhist	Islamic	Sinic	Buddhist	Islamic

Table 4 Two overlapping markers

	Ethnic Laos in Thailand (1893–)			Ethnic Chinese in Thailand (1900s–)	
	Minority	Hegemon		Minority	Hegemon
Language	Lao	Central Thai	*Language*	Chinese	Central Thai
Religion	Buddhism	Buddhism	*Religion*	Buddhism	Buddhism
Phenotype	Phenotype 1	Phenotype 1	*Phenotype*	Phenotype 1	Phenotype 1

hegemon will use the state to seek integration of the minority. The minority will also perceive the malleability of ethnicity. Due to the willingness from both sides to overlook differences, ethnic integration can occur.

In this section we consider two minorities that have been successfully integrated in Thailand (see **Table 4**). First, the largest minority in the country are the ethnic Lao. They are concentrated in northeastern Thailand, comprising approximately 28% of the country's population. Even though this group still refers to itself as Lao among coethnics (Saowanee and McCargo 2014), large proportions avoid identification as Lao. Instead, they favor being identified as Thai – often with the moniker *Isan*, a borrowed Pali word meaning northeasterner (Keyes 2014; Ricks 2019). Indeed, in a 2020 survey of 400 people from the region, only 13% identified themselves as either Lao or Thai–Lao; the remaining 87% choose to identify as Isan (Ricks 2021). This pattern is not wholly surprising: The Thai state actively developed this terminology to reduce the threat that such a large ethnic minority might pose for the central Thai state (Draper and Peerasit 2018; Iijima 2018).

The second group is the Sino-Thais: namely, ethnic Chinese who have negotiated their Chinese ancestry while identifying as Thai. Here, the boundaries of the Thai identity have been malleable enough to allow the overseas Chinese populations to become Thai by adopting the Thai language and cultural practices. Indeed, multiple popular and powerful figures in Thai politics are Thais with Chinese ancestry. Examples include the prime ministers Chuan Leekpai, Abhisit Vejjajjiva, and the Shinawatra siblings Thaksin and Yingluck. The royal family also boasts Chinese ethnic ties. This vital and influential population in Thailand is widely accepted as "Thai" – a stark contrast to the Chinese communities in other parts of Southeast Asia (as we will see in subsequent sections). The integration of these two distinct groups demonstrates the importance of emphasizing multiple overlapping cleavages, wherein both the minority and the hegemon can come to see the former as part of the latter.

Ethnic Lao in Thailand

By the mid-1800s, Lao people inhabited both sides of the Mekong River, comprising much of the population across the area that is present-day Northeast Thailand. In the late 1700s, the Siamese had conquered the Lao kingdoms of Luang Prabang and Vientiane, resulting in the forcible relocation of many Lao to the area known today as central Thailand to serve as labor for the Siamese. Additional Lao were encouraged – if not compelled – to relocate their families and villages to Siamese territory (Breazeale 1975). The resettlement of Lao meant that when the border between French Indochina and Siam solidified, the Lao population to the west of the Mekong was many times larger than that which remained to the east.

While Lao kingdoms and regional elites were vassals of the Siamese palace, they enjoyed relative autonomy until the 1860s. Conflicts with the French forced the Siamese state to aggressively establish control over the region during the late nineteenth century (Breazeale 1975; Thongchai 1994; Vickery 1970). Initially, there was some Lao resistance. In 1901/1902, an armed rebellion linked to millennial religious beliefs developed; the better-armed Siamese brutally suppressed the rebellion (Murdoch 1974). For the Siamese state, military dominance over the Lao coincided with increased concern about the potential of a Lao–Thai ethnic conflict. While the Lao people's military capacity was weak, the Siamese palace feared that the French could exploit the Lao ethnicity on both sides of the Mekong, thereby justifying suzerainty claims over portions of the Khorat Plateau.

The Lao language – part of the Tai-Kadai linguistic family – was distinct from the Thai-speaking Siamese. They practiced different cultural and political traditions. Although the Lao sangha (Buddhist priesthood) was of the Theravada tradition, it was separate from that of the Siamese tradition (Kamala 1997). Indeed, the Siamese generally considered the Lao a different race – one that was supposedly inferior to the Siamese (Ricks 2021). The Lao had also long been treated as enemies of the Siamese kingdom, who, once conquered, could be carried away as slaves to serve their military masters. In essence, prior to 1900, the Siamese state recognized the Lao as a distinct ethnic group (Keyes 1997; Streckfuss 1993).

This changed in 1893 in response to a disastrous military engagement with the French. French gunboats anchored outside the Siamese palace, threatening to depose the monarchy. The treaty to end hostilities provided extraterritorial rights to all French citizens *and* denizens of French Indochina – including Khmer, Lao, and Vietnamese people. This gave the Lao in the Siamese territory the opportunity to become French subjects; indeed, some began carrying French flags and purchasing letters to declare themselves French protégé (Strate 2015).

King Chulalongkorn's palace administration responded with a campaign to eradicate any designation of the Lao people west of the Mekong as Lao. Instead, they would be referred to as fellow Thais. Officials took great pains to remove the Lao reference, including abolishing Lao as a category on all official censuses since 1905 (Grabowsky 1996). All Lao people were henceforth identified as Thai (see also Draper and Peerasit 2018).

The term Lao had also previously been applied to three administrative regions (*monthon*). However, this appellation was removed in favor of directional names based on their location relative to Bangkok. A new term emerged: Isan (literally, "northeast") was initially used for the administrative region that had formerly been called *Monthon Lao Kao* (White Lao Circle) and covered the region of the Khorat Plateau that today includes Ubon Ratchathani and Roi Et provinces (Iijima 2018). Later, in the 1920s, the term Isan was applied to the entire northeast region; and, over time, it became a frequent appellation for the people of the area. Rather than referring to the Lao (*khon lao*), the state termed them Isan people (*khon isan*) as a subset of Thais. This shift would replace their ethnic identity with a directional (or regional) one. In essence, Lao people of Thailand began to be called "northeastern people."

Today, there remains group identification among ethnic Lao (Saowanee and McCargo 2014, 2019; also see McCargo and Krisadawan 2004). However, after a century of integration policies, the Lao people of the Khorat Plateau have adopted a Thai identity – through both the education system and the Bangkok-based market economy (Keyes 2014). Likewise, Ricks (2019, 2021) finds evidence that Lao-speaking people of Thailand see themselves as Thai and prefer a regional identity rather than to be linked to the Lao ethnic identity – at least when interacting with outsiders.

We have evidence that ethnic identification was abandoned during the first half of the twentieth century. With the fall of the absolute monarchy (1932), political organizations emerged to promote the welfare of the northeastern inhabitants. These organizations – along with their leaders – took pains to identify as Thai and to focus on regionalism rather than separatism (Keyes 2014: 64–89). Even the Communist Party of Thailand actively portrayed itself as distinctly Thai, rather than part of a larger transnational, Southeast Asian communist organization (Somchai 2002).

One major factor in the ethnic Lao successfully merging into the broader Thai identity has been the sharing of multiple ethnic markers – per our theory. This means that the ethnic boundary between the Lao and the Thai is porous and relatively flexible. Ethnic Lao in Thailand share both religion and phenotype with their Thai counterparts. The main marker that distinguishes the two ethnicities is language. We address each of these in turn.

First, both Lao and Thai people are largely adherents to Theravada Buddhism. When integration efforts began, the practices of Theravada Buddhism between the two populations were distinct. Following reforms by King Mongkut (1851–1868) – who had spent more than two decades as a monk – the palace brought the Siamese sangha under greater control (see Reynolds 1973). Conversely, the Lao tradition of village monks followed different practices – namely, being more concerned with the community, including participating in manual labor, providing education to villagers, and taking part in local festivals and dramatic performances (Kamala 1997: 23–40). The actions of the village monks were problematic and potentially disruptive for the Siamese state, especially as village temples were often the main source of education for Lao children.

The Siamese state, however, was able to exert control over Buddhist institutions. This was done first by centralizing authority over the sangha under the direction of the Siamese palace. In 1902, the palace propagated the Education Act. The new legislation removed the responsibility for education from the monks. The monks who continued educating children were forced to adopt the state curriculum (Reynolds 1973; Wyatt 1966). Furthermore, the authority to appoint monks was centralized. Monks who rebelled against this development were sent to Bangkok for retraining. While Chiang Mai's Khruubaa Srivichai was the most famous detained monk (Bowie 2014), many Lao abbots from the northeast were forced to resolve their differences with the centralized Siamese sangha (Kamala 1997). Within a few short years, the Buddhist priesthood throughout the country was largely brought under the control of Bangkok. In sum, while some local practices persist, the religion of the minority Lao and the hegemon (central) Thai has become relatively uniform, making religion a unifying characteristic rather than a potential point of contention.

Second, the Thai and Lao people do not vary greatly in terms of appearance – in other words, phenotype is not a distinguishing marker between the two. Although there is some genetic evidence that the people of Isan and people in and around Bangkok form distinct genetic subgroups, both groups derive from a common "major ancestry" (Pongsakorn et al. 2013). Additionally, the genetic composition of Thailand's central region is diverse. Notably, large proportions of the population share the same genetic grouping as Isan people – meaning the genetic variation is unlikely to produce stark phenotypical distinctions between them (Pongsakorn et al. 2013). As this genetic research is recent, there may be an argument that differences were more pronounced in the past. This is suspect, however, as French explorers in the late 1800s were divided on distinctions between the Lao and the Siamese, with one noting that "Laotians greatly resembled the Siamese" (Aymonier 2000: 67). It is important to remember that the French had an interest in differentiating between the two groups; thus, such comments suggest that the groups were quite similar (see Streckfuss 1993).

While Thai nationals today commonly claim they can identify the regional origins of people based on appearance, these assertions are often based on social class rather than phenotype per se. For instance, some Thai nationals claim Isan people are darker in complexion than those from the north or central plains. This plays into a social hierarchy that privileges Thais from Bangkok and the central region, and those from the romanticized northern provinces (Sophorntavy 2017: 122–123). In truth, the darker complexion stereotypically assigned to Isan people has more to do with exposure to the sun through farming or performing manual labor than any widespread phenotypical distinction. Many people who hail from Isan but now work in Bangkok blend relatively seamlessly with the natives of the metropolis. Phenotypical markers – such as eye shape, hair color, or body type – are not typically distinct between ethnic Lao and Thais. Thus, there are no true physical markers that can be used to reliably identify a person as either a coethnic or a member of the out-group.

Language remains the main marker of Lao ethnicity in Thailand. While both Lao and Thai are members of the Tai-Kadai language family, the two are distinct tongues (Lewis et al. 2016; see also Smalley 1994).[7] They are mutually unintelligible without some training or exposure. Today, however, there is a great deal of cross-exposure between the two – although native Lao speakers on both sides of the Mekong River are much more familiar with central Thai than native Thai speakers are with Lao. Many native Lao speakers can understand spoken Thai, while relatively few native Thai speakers can understand Lao sans assistance.

We do not have comprehensive linguistic data for the time when Chulalongkorn's government began to consolidate Siamese control over the Khorat Plateau and delineate the borders of Siam with French Indochina. There are, however, estimates suggesting that more than half of the population spoke either Lao or Khammuang (the language spoken in the north), while only about 15 percent spoke central Thai at home (Keyes 2003: 181). The Siamese state actively sought to erase the linguistic Lao–Thai distinctions (Iijima 2018; Ricks 2021). Centralized education focused on promoting literacy in standard Thai.

---

[7] Enfield (2002) argues that these distinctions should not be thought of as clear borders; there is substantial variation within both Lao and Thai languages. Moreover, the distinctions between the languages are politically promoted.

Moreover, many ethnic Lao willingly learned the national tongue to access economic opportunities (Diller 2002; Keyes 2014). Even so, language remains the major identifier of the ethnic Lao minority in Thailand today. Approximately one-third of Thailand's population still speaks it as their native tongue (Suwilai et al. 2004; Lewis et al. 2016). However, more than a century of assimilation efforts has blurred this identifier. The Lao spoken in Thailand has drifted closer to Thai through both education and exposure to Bangkok media. Additionally, the Thai state refers to the Lao tongue spoken in Thailand as Isan language (*phasa Isan*), further diluting the distinctiveness of Lao. Both Lao Thai and central Thai have largely accepted each other as fellow nationals, glossing over their separate ethnic identities.

Thus, the ethnic boundary separating the Lao and the Thai is a weak one based primarily on linguistic differences. The ethnic difference was much stronger prior to the Thai state's integration efforts that began under Chulalongkorn in the late nineteenth century. However, as the hegemon has pursued integration strategies due to shared characteristics between the Thai and the Lao, the disparity between the two groups has diminished. In sum, as our theory predicts, the integration of the minority Lao into the Thai identity has been largely successful because of the cross-cutting ethnic markers between the two groups. The integration of the Lao minority in Thailand, then, provides a clear case where a permeable boundary has contributed to integration.

Ethnic Chinese in Thailand

Throughout Southeast Asia, the overseas Chinese population has faced serious challenges and exclusionary treatment in the process of nation-building (Suryadinata 1997; Wang 2004). One exception is Thailand, where Chinese immigrants have become deeply integrated. On the part of the native Thais, the ethnic Chinese are well accepted, admired for their economic success, and celebrated as political leaders. For their part, the ethnic Chinese have also willingly integrated, adopting "Thai-ness." While they remember their Chinese heritage, they also promote and proclaim pride in the Thai nation (see, e.g., Chaun 2010; Kasian 2009). Thus, the Chinese in Thailand serve as a second example of integration of a minority.[8]

Significant immigration by ethnic Chinese into Siam occurred in the latter half of the nineteenth century and into the twentieth. By that time, however, Chinese-descent individuals were already well-placed in Thai society, including

---

[8] While Skinner (1957, 1960) argued that the ethnic Chinese assimilated into Thai society, more recent scholars (Chan and Tong 1993; Lee 2014; Morita 2007) have argued that Skinner failed to acknowledge the persistence of Chineseness among many Sino-Thais. Thus, we avoid the term "assimilation and" instead favor "integration."

the palace. Demand for labor drew Chinese to Thailand, while overpopulation, war, and famine drove them to leave their homes. Skinner (1957: 79) estimates that by 1910, 9.5% of the total Siam population was either immigrant Chinese (3.91%) or local-born people of Chinese descent (5.59%). The ethnic Chinese were largely concentrated in and around Bangkok, where up to half of the population was either Chinese or of Chinese descent. From the 1910s, Chinese immigration boomed, before falling to only a trickle following World War II. By the 1950s, the ethnic Chinese population stood at 11–12% of the total population (Skinner 1957: 183). One source estimates that in 2011 up to 14% of Thailand's total population was of Chinese descent (Lee 2014).

Counting Chinese ethnics in Thailand is difficult, however. Many immigrants and their children have integrated so well with the general population that it can be difficult to distinguish ethnicities. Indeed, as Skinner (1957: 187) notes, "The difficulty of telling Chinese from Thai in Lower Siam where a large section of the Thai population have Chinese blood is obvious; some of the most 'Thai' families are racially up to three-quarters Chinese." Thai laws after the early 1900s did not distinguish between Chinese and Thai ethnicities. This allowed children born of Chinese and Thai unions (*lukjin*) to utilize both identities: being Thai when advantageous, while retaining links to their Chinese heritage. Perhaps most importantly, limitations on Chinese schools forced children to take part in the Thai education system, thus molding students into a standard Thai identity.

Integration, however, was not always guaranteed. Indeed, the nineteenth century saw uprisings by Chinese immigrants (1824 in Chanthaburi, 1842 in Nakhon Chai Sri, 1845 in Lang Suan, and the 1848 sugar refinery rebellions); riots in Bangkok (1869, 1883, 1889, and 1895); and abuse of extraterritoriality by ethnic Chinese. The Chinese also dominated the market economy, which could have easily spurred ethnic tensions. Instead, integration efforts were taken by both the Chinese community and the Thai elites. The result was a process whereby both sides took steps to reduce ethnic distance for their mutual benefit (Wasana 2019). Today, tension between the Sino–Thai and Thai communities is negligible.

The Chinese became Thai through Thailand's process of nation-building. Wasana (2019) argues that integration was most successful among the Chinese elites, as the working-class Chinese were susceptible to discrimination and exclusion. Nonetheless, most ethnic Chinese living in Thailand see themselves as Thai. As was the case with the ethnic Lao, the development of nationalism was a top-down process: It involved convincing (1) the ethnic Chinese that they could be Thai; and (2) the rest of the Thai that the distinctions were minimal. Unlike the Lao minority, however, this process was more contentious, and included significant public derision of the ethnic Chinese community during the early 1900s.

The most famous example of this occurred during the reign of King Vajiravudh (1910–1925). The King penned an anti-Chinese tract titled *The Jews of the Orient* (1914), as well as many other public denunciations of the Chinese. The essay, which was available in both Thai and English, borrowed from Western antisemitism in its attack on the Chinese community in Thailand. The argument was that the ethnic Chinese were more loyal to their homeland or their community than they were to Siam (Vella 1978: 202–204). The claim was embedded in Siam's emerging sense of national-ism – which incorporated elements of national shame due to extraterritoriality and loss of land to Western colonialists (Strate 2015) – coupled with fears that the ethnic Chinese were dominating the market economy. Indeed, many ethnic Chinese in Siam had declared themselves European subjects to take advantage of extraterritoriality provisions. Wasana (2019) argues that Vajiravudh's efforts were intended to convince these ethnic Chinese – especially the *lukjin* – to become loyal to the monarchy. While the king engaged the ethnic Chinese through the press and other means, he chose not to antagonize them with laws.

Conversely, the post-monarchy (1932) governments were much harsher toward the ethnic Chinese, especially that of Field Marshall Phibulsongkram (Phibun). Phibun promoted ultranationalist measures to force integration into a central Thai identity (Kobkua 1995). This included twelve cultural mandates, compulsory "Thai-ification" of the economy, and a series of anti-Chinese laws and decrees. Chinese schools were closed or compelled to teach in Thai, requiring ethnic Chinese children to learn to speak, read, and write in Thai. The end of extraterritoriality also forced ethnic Chinese to choose either Chinese or Thai citizenship. Skinner (1957: 381) observed that without school-ing in their ancestral language, the ethnic Chinese no longer identified as Chinese. Indeed, many Chinese willingly chose to integrate as Thais to take advantage of the sociopolitical benefits that were afforded with said identity (Skinner 1960).

While Chinese identities still exist in Thai society, the group has adopted the Thai national identity (Kasian 2009), and the Thai population has largely accepted the Chinese community in Thailand as Thai. In fact, if we consider Thailand's democratically elected prime ministers over the past three decades, all have some Chinese ancestry: Chuan Leekpai, Banharn Silpa-archa, Chavalit Yongchaiyudh, Thaksin Shinawatra, Samak Sundaravej, Somchai Wongsawat, Abhisit Vejjajiva, and Yingluck Shinawatra. Moreover, the extremely popular Shinawatra siblings, Thaksin and Yingluck, have proudly displayed their

Chinese heritage, including public visits to their ancestral hometown in Guangdong. Beyond this, the royals have significant Chinese ancestry (for estimates, see Skinner 1957: 26). Members of the royal family, such as Princess Sirindhorn, have officially supported links with the Chinese community both in Thailand and in China. Since the 1990s, Thai elites have also promoted the image of Thailand and China as siblings (*phinong kan*), thereby improving the public perception and acceptance of the ethnic Chinese (Pongphisoot 2016).

We see, then, that the Thai government and elites sought to assimilate ethnic Chinese within the Thai identity. We also see that the ethnic Chinese have chosen to integrate. How does this relate to our theoretical expectations? First, religious distinctions between the two groups are relatively porous. Thai religious practices, as noted, are dominantly Theravada Buddhist, but practices are relatively flexible. On the other hand, Chinese immigrants to Thailand practice both Mahayana Buddhism and Confucian philosophy, mixing in reverence for ancestors. The question, then, is whether these religious practices would be sufficiently distinct to separate the groups. The answer is no. Early immigrants from China easily adapted to Thai Buddhist practices, worshiping at Thai Buddhist *wat* (temples) and donating alms to Buddhist monks. They also engaged with the animist traditions of the Siamese, including reverencing symbols such as the city pillar (*lak muang*) and animist spirits (*phi*). The boundaries of the two styles of Buddhism were porous (Skinner 1957). Many ethnic Chinese also accommodated and adapted to Thai beliefs – for example, entering the monkhood, practicing cremation rather than burial (Boonsanong 1971), and holding funerals within Thai Buddhist temples (Hill 1992).

For their part, Thailand's version of Buddhist practice is syncretic, porous, and sometimes hybridized – at least as popularly practiced (Pattana 2005; Reynolds 1973). This allows Thais to practice and adopt alternative religious practices without seeing such behavior as sinful or taboo. Many Thais also adopted ethnic Chinese religious practices, such as ancestor worship and praying to Chinese deities. Festivals, including the Chinese New Year, are regularly celebrated by those who are not of Chinese ancestry. Due to both the adaptability of the Chinese immigrants and the receptivity of Thailand's religious practices, there is no hard and fast differentiation between the two. While the ethnic Chinese do maintain religious cultural practices, these do not preclude community members from taking part in Thai religious practices – nor Thais from taking part in Chinese practices. In short, religion does not separate the two communities.

Second, based on appearance, the ethnic Chinese and native Thais of Thailand exhibit relatively slight phenotypical differences that do not create a barrier to intermingling. As Skinner (1957: 128) claims, "Differences in physical appearance between Thai and Chinese are not marked, and if anything the Thai show a preference for certain physical characteristics – fair skin especially – more typical of Chinese than of 'pure-blooded' Thai." Boonsanong (1971: 70) noted that physical appearance cannot be a clear marker of ethnicity since natives of Thailand cannot rely on looks to differentiate the two groups. Relatedly, the Thai hierarchy that privileges urbanized and lighter-skinned appearances benefits the descendants of Chinese immigrants whose skin tone reflects desirable characteristics portrayed in Thai media (see also Sophorntavy 2017: 122–123). Importantly, by the time of Chulalongkorn, when the hegemon began to cultivate a Thai ethnic and national identity, the hegemon elites (including the royal family) all had some Chinese ancestry – but they ruled over a kingdom of people who did not appear Chinese. They also faced colonial threats from the British and the French, who emphasized the importance of ethnic identity. The Thai hegemon thus created a Thai identity which included a phenotype with relatively loose boundaries.[9] In other words, there is a spectrum of acceptable phenotypes that can be considered "Thai," including those who may appear Chinese. Callahan (2003: 495) notes that even when anti-Chinese sentiment does occur, it is often met with fiercely nationalist rhetoric by Thais of Chinese ancestry, and "people have to work hard to make distinctions between the Chinese, Thai, and Sino-Thai populations."

Additionally, any physical distinctions between ethnic Chinese and Thai have become diluted through intermarriages over the past two centuries. The *lukjin* became a prominent portion of the ethnic Chinese community at the turn of the twentieth century; moreover, the Thai census considers many of these racially "Thai" unless they identified themselves otherwise (Skinner 1957). Thus, according to phenotype, we cannot reliably distinguish ethnic Chinese in Thailand.

This leaves us with language as the primary marker to differentiate the ethnic Chinese community in Thailand (Boonsanong 1971). Chinese and Thai languages are mutually unintelligible, with the two languages belonging to separate language families: Sino-Tibetan and Tai-Kadai, respectively. Indeed, language remains the main marker that continues to identify the Chinese community today (Lee 2014). Language – and the links it provided to the Chinese homeland via print and schools – was a point of friction in the first half of the twentieth century (Skinner 1957). Thai elites, however, did not see this as a barrier to Chinese integration. Instead, they pursued a series of policies

---

[9] This is in sharp contrast to the colonial powers who emphasized boundaries based on physical appearance (see our discussion of Malaysia and Singapore in Section 3).

to encourage (often forcibly) the ethnic Chinese to learn and adopt Thai (Wasana 2019).

For their part, the ethnic Chinese also saw this single ethnic marker as a relatively low hurdle to enter Thai society. Many willingly learned Thai to take advantage of benefits in both the state and the market. Some completely assimilated as Thais (Skinner 1957, 1960). Others have retained their ethnic identity through language (Chan and Tong 1993). Today, many Sino-Thais are bilingual, although there is some movement toward more extensive use of Thai in daily life among second-generation (if not higher) descendants of Chinese immigrants (Lee 2014). In sum, language alone serves as a vital marker of ethnic Chinese identity in Thailand. The hegemon Thai, especially the elites, attempted to integrate the ethnic Chinese into the Thai identity – a process that began in the early 1900s and continues today through the education system. The Chinese in Thailand have largely merged their ethnic identity within a Thai national identity, even though the continued use of Chinese languages acts as a distinct identity marker.

Conclusion

Through the examples of the Lao and the Chinese in Thailand, we see that when ethnic identities have multiple overlapping markers – for example, phenotype and religion – the border between two ethnicities can become porous. Without an additional marker to differentiate themselves, the Lao and the Chinese become "Thai" – with ample support and coercion from the hegemon. In both cases, the Thai state focused on integration efforts through the education system. Education was forced in the Thai language to overcome the only marker that separated the groups. The state did not need to convert the ethnic minority to a new faith; nor was it compelled to convince the rest of the population to overlook phenotypic differences. Language education alone was the challenge. For their part, the Lao and the Chinese have been able to accept the Thai language and see themselves as being Thai.

It should be noted that both cases overlap on the same two markers. This might cause some pause as to whether linguistic barriers are easier to overcome than religious or phenotypical ones. First, distinctions between religions could provide a clear foundation for exclusion. One possible counterexample to this is the predominantly Muslim population found in Satun province in Thailand. That group – once self-identified as Malay – now sees itself as Thai (Parks 2009). This population shares two characteristics – language and phenotype – with the politically dominant Thai. Beyond Satun, in and around Bangkok, we also see Islamic populations that have become Thai through their adoption of the Thai language and by being accepted within the broadly defined Thai phenotype (Van Roy 2016; Winyu 2014). In short, the Islam–Buddhism religious distinction alone has not prevented integration into the Thai national identity.

Second, research indicates that physical distinctions, such as phenotype, are socially malleable (Wimmer 2013: 7–10). This suggests that if phenotype were taken alone as an ethnic marker, it could be overcome. Horowitz (1971: 243) argued that phenotype or color "can also be inaccurate and misleading" as a marker. Indeed, the Chinese in Thailand are an example where phenotype could have become a dividing characteristic; however, due to historical intermixing of native Thais and Chinese immigrants, the phenotypical distinctions are minimized. As stated, the intermingling of Chinese immigrants and Thai elites prior to the time of Chulalongkorn created a situation in which the hegemon had strong incentives to craft a Thai identity that allowed for the acceptability of a broad range of phenotypes. Thus, the "Thai" phenotype is a broad tent that can include those who appear Chinese, the mixed *lukjin*, the Lao of Isan, and – as we will discuss – the Malay community in the south.

This discussion suggests that what matters for integration is not *which* markers are shared but *how many*. In Section 4, we will return to another ethnic group in Thailand and to the ethnic Chinese in another country – and we will see that in both of these cases the outcome has been violent contention.

3 Ethnic Accommodation

In this section, we examine what happens when the minority and the hegemon share no ethnic markers. Our theory predicts that when no cross-cutting cleavages exist, integration is not possible. There is no ethnic mechanism for the minority to identify with the hegemon – that is, they are not able to see themselves as members of the same in-group. For the hegemon, one option is to engage in violence and repression, as we saw in Indonesia with the Chinese during Suharto (see Section 1). But if the hegemon is trying to avoid conflict, the only option available is **accommodation**: that is, *the legal acknowledgment of minority distinctiveness and institutional efforts to manage the differences*. In this section, we focus on this latter option.

In Southeast Asia, at least two ethnic groups share no overlap on our three ethnic markers: the Chinese and the Malays. While the Chinese language is technically an amalgamation of vernaculars, it belongs to the Sino-Tibetan language family. Conversely, the Malay language – also a collection of different vernaculars – is part of the Austronesian language family. And although there are some Chinese words, mostly food (e.g., *mi* and *teh*), in the Malay lexicon, there is minimal intelligibility between the two languages (Hamilton 1924). Likewise, there is also little religious overlap between the Chinese and the Malays. The Chinese are predominantly Buddhists – at least historically. In the contemporary period, the Protestant population is substantial thanks to European proselytizing efforts (Amrith 2011; Leow 2016). Conversely, the Malays are overwhelmingly Sunni Muslims (Ali 2008; Andaya and Andaya 2017) – an association that has been legally recognized by the governments in Brunei, Indonesia, Malaysia, and Singapore (Fox 2008). Finally, when it comes to phenotype, there is a notable difference between the two groups. The Chinese are descendants of immigrants from (mostly southern) China, with a lighter skin tone (Skinner 1950). Conversely, the Malays are indigenous to Southeast Asia: "son of the soil" (*bumiputera*). The wide-held stereotype is that Malays have darker skin (Ibrahim et al. 2010). While appearance-based distinctions are rarely indisputable, the differences are relatively conspicuous, especially when reinforced by the (British) colonial authority obsessed with physical and social segregation (Hirschman 1986; Kim 2020).

The lack of shared markers between the Chinese and the Malays allows us to examine the politics of ethnic accommodation. Here, Malaysia and Singapore are a natural paired comparison (see **Table 5**). Both countries were colonized by the British, and hence the same racial categories were recognized and heavily institutionalized (Malays, Chinese, Indians, and Eurasians/Others). Today, the ethnolinguistic diversity of the two countries mirrors each other. The likelihood that any two people chosen at random will speak different languages is 74.7% in Malaysia and 77.3% in Singapore (Lewis, Simons, and Fenning 2016).

Table 5 No overlapping markers

	Ethnic Chinese in Malaysia (1957–)			*Ethnic Malays in Singapore* (1965–)	
	Minority	**Hegemon**		**Minority**	**Hegemon**
Language	Chinese	Malay	*Language*	Malay	Chinese
Religion	Buddhism	Islam	*Religion*	Islam	Buddhism/ Christianity/ Mixed
Phenotype	Phenotype 1	Phenotype 2	*Phenotype*	Phenotype 1	Phenotype 2

In both Malaya[10] and Singapore, an anticommunist, multiracial hegemonic party (coalition) came to power pre-independence. While the political landscape has experienced some major turbulence since then, we continue to see ethnic accommodation in both countries. In Malaysia, the government coalition has always included at least one Chinese party. And for some time, the ethnic Chinese held several key ministerial portfolios (e.g., the finance ministry from independence until 1974). And culturally, the Chinese language is a medium of instruction for public schools at the primary level. There are 1,297 Chinese language primary schools today in Malaysia (Wu 2021). Likewise, in Singapore, Malays are numerically represented in the government, including the largely ceremonial office of the president – which was legally earmarked for ethnic Malay candidates in 2017's election process. Malay is the singular national language: It is used in the national anthem and the state motto. It is also one of the four official languages of the state. Additionally, Islam is protected per the constitution; the Mosque Building Fund was established to finance the building and upgrading of new and existing mosques (Ibrahim 1999). The accommodation of the Chinese in Malaysia and of the Malays in Singapore is testament to how governments can be constrained to accommodate minorities when there is no overlapping ethnic cleavage. We will see, however, that this accommodation manifests in different ways between the two countries.

Ethnic Chinese in Malaysia

In the aftermath of World War II, Malay nationalists formed the United Malays National Organization (UMNO) as they sought to negotiate independence from the British. UMNO was different from the other Malay parties with its non-anti-imperialist (i.e., it did not call for the radical, immediate expulsion of the British) and noncommunist positions. In fact, on this latter point, UMNO cooperated with the colonial authorities to defeat the communist insurgency. And while the British were sympathetic to UMNO and willing to grant independence, UMNO – led by Tunku Abdul Rahman (henceforth the Tunku) – feared that the colonial authorities would suspend negotiations upon signs of ethnic tensions.

Consequently, UMNO leaders negotiated with – if not outright accommodated – the Chinese minority. The 1957 Malaya census identified 37 percent of the peninsula's inhabitants as Chinese, with high concentrations in the urban centers (namely Kuala Lumpur and neighboring Selangor, Johor, Penang, and Perak). The Chinese dominance in the urban areas was due to immigration

---

[10] Malaya would become Malaysia in 1963 upon merging with Singapore, Sarawak, and North Borneo.

settlement patterns and their role as middle merchants (Amrith 2011). It was also the result of British policies during the Malayan Emergency. As part of the campaign against the communist guerillas who were based in the jungles, the British interned large rural communities in urban settlements known as New Villages. The forced relocation of the predominant ethnic Chinese not only deprived the communists of recruits, it also created concentrated Chinese pockets in urban areas (Strauch 1981).

Two parties vied to represent the Chinese in Malaya. One was the Malayan (later renamed Malaysian) Communist Party (MCP) that was supported – both in military logistics and in morale – by Mao Zedong and the Chinese Communist Party (Chin 2004). The other was the Malayan (later renamed Malaysian) Chinese Association (MCA) – led by English-educated business elites with financial and recruitment support from Chiang Kai-Shek and the Kuomintang (Heng 1988; Yong and McKenna 1990). Given the ideological preferences of all relevant parties – including that of London – UMNO and MCA formed an alliance (Rahman Putra al-Haji 1978).

The negotiations initially produced electoral cooperation in the 1952 Kuala Lumpur municipal council elections. The two parties agreed to avoid contesting the same seats; instead, the party that did not field a candidate in that district would direct its supporters to vote for the candidate from the partner party. The result was astounding: The UMNO–MCA coalition won nine of the twelve seats. In 1955, UMNO and MCA formalized their coalition as the Alliance Party (with the Malayan Indian Congress party as a third member) to contest the Legislative Council election. The Alliance Party would go on to win all but one of the fifty-two seats.

As the Alliance Party looked to secure independence, each member recognized that any sign of ethnic tension could result in the British suspending negotiations. For the Malays, there were three issues that were not negotiable: the status of the Malay language as the national (and official) language, the status of Islam as the official religion, and the recognition of the Malay people with special privileges. The Chinese gained nothing from acquiescing to these three demands and integrating with the Malays. In fact, Chinese preferences would be undermined with each one – for example, they wanted the use of Chinese vernaculars in schools.

The Tunku and UMNO recognized that integration of the Chinese was neither possible nor desirable for the Malays. The Malay leaders, however, also understood that without giving concessions to the Chinese, there would be no Malayan state. To this end, what we see is a collective compromise – namely, ethnic accommodation. While the Malays got their demands, the Chinese received compensation. Chinese was a recognized language of education;

English was also afforded the status of an official language – albeit temporarily. In exchange for acknowledging the special privileges of the Malays, the Chinese would be granted immediate citizenship – a radical proposition at the time. And finally, given the Chinese dominance in the economy, UMNO agreed to let the Chinese retain their economic positions – as long as the Malays had a larger influence in politics (Liu 2015b).

The de jure accommodation of the Chinese has largely remained in equilibrium since independence. The extent of accommodation (i.e., the de facto recognition) however, has oscillated over four critical junctures – frequently to the chagrin of the ethnic Chinese. At each juncture, there was a shift in the political landscape, thereby altering the minority–hegemon relationship. When power dynamics change, how ethnic accommodation manifests can change as well. Yet, it is important to note that through these junctures, there is still a clear preference for accommodation rather than attempting integration. This is evident in that both groups have demonstrated beliefs of a fixed, immutable boundary between the Chinese and Malays.

The first critical juncture took place in May 1969. Leading up to the May 10 elections, UMNO faced challenges from more radical pro-Malay parties who felt the Tunku had conceded too much to the Chinese. Likewise, the MCA faced threats from other opposition Chinese and mixed-race parties. The Democratic Action Party (DAP), for example, championed racial equality – a position the MCA had sacrificed to be in the governing coalition *and* to secure independence. Although the Alliance Party won a legislative majority, its margin of victory was small. Additionally, MCA's electoral defeat in the Chinese constituent districts enflamed ethnic tensions. When riots broke out, the government imposed a state of emergency, thereby suspending parliament. During this suspension, deputy prime minister Abdul Razak replaced the Tunku as head of government. When parliament reconvened in 1971, the Chinese found their political representation within the new government coalition (*Barisan Nasional* or National Front) to be marginal at best. In contrast to the Alliance Party – "born out of necessity of the three major races to work together to fulfill the prerequisite set by the British for negotiating independence" (Abdul Samad 1998: 118) – the UMNO-dominated National Front – a oversized coalition of more than ten parties – "came to life as the savior of a nation on the brink of collapse" (Abdul Samad 1998: 118).

The second critical juncture was the 1987 party election for the UMNO general assembly, which resulted in a split within the party and the consolidation of the (more) Malay nationalist faction. Leading one faction (Team A) was Dr. Mahathir bin Mohamad, the incumbent prime minister. Mahathir had always been wary of the ethnic Chinese, describing initial efforts toward a multiethnic coalition as the result of "the Malay fear of losing out to the Chinese" (Mahathir 1970: 10). Leading the other faction (Team B) was Tunku Razaleigh Hamzah. Razaleigh courted (amongst other constituent groups) the DAP – an opposition party that by now had the support of the majority of the Chinese population (Khong 1991). The rivalry descended into "militant" jockeying for Malay votes and "demeaning" the Chinese – both symbolically and substantively (Case 1991: 467). As tensions escalated – setting off the hoarding of basic goods – Mahathir invoked the Internal Security Act (ISA). Under the ISA, he detained his "rivals" – both intra- and intercommunal – thereby putting to rest ethnic tensions (Slater 2003; also see Case 1991).

The third critical juncture was the defeat of the National Front in the 2018 election. The Alliance of Hope's (*Pakatan Harapan*: PH) historic victory not only ushered in Mahathir's second stint as prime minister, it also saw expanded Chinese political representation through the DAP. With PH's electoral success, DAP's Lim Guang Eng was appointed finance minister – a highly coveted, symbolic portfolio for the Chinese. It was a portfolio the ethnic Chinese had held until 1974. And while Lim identified first and foremost as Malaysian, the Chinese community saw his appointment as something to celebrate (*China Qiaowang* 2018). It was a commitment to racial equality and "a return to meritocracy" (Leong 2018).

The shift toward a "New Malaysia" would galvanize nationalist Malays who believed accommodation had gone too far (*Aliran* 2019). UMNO and PAS tapped into this resentment, managing to peel away disgruntled parties within PH, resulting in government collapse in February 2020. This is the fourth critical juncture. The new coalition, the National Alliance (*Perikatan Nasional*: PN), assumed power in March 2020. PN has cast itself as a protector of Malay interests. The Malay dominance is evident within the cabinet portfolios: There is only one Chinese minister in the cabinet (MCA's Wee Ka Siong as transport minister) – the fewest and the lowest-ranked portfolio for the ethnic Chinese in Malaysian history.

Prior to the 2018 PH victory, we see a gradual erosion of Chinese accommodation. In 1972, the government removed English as an official language, citing that its temporary status had expired. In its stead, Malay became the sole language of government services. Likewise, English language schools were gradually converted into Malay language institutions (Burhanudeen 2006; Liu 2015a). Islam remained the official state religion. And finally, the special privileges afforded to the Malays (*bumiputera* generally) were further expanded through the New Economic Plan – including quotas (floors) for bank loans and government employment for the Malays and caps (ceilings) for enterprises and university admissions for the Chinese (Esman 1987). To solidify these changes – and to "put a lid on the passionate debate on language policies" (Lee HG 2007: 132) – the UMNO-dominated National Front (*Barisan Nasional*: BN) adopted an amendment in 1971 to the Sedition Act making it a punishable offense to question language policies, the position of Islam, and the special status of the Malay people.

Note that while there was de jure accommodation, there were also de facto restrictions – including limiting the number of Chinese primary schools (Lee HG 2007). This limitation created severe overcrowding in Chinese schools, with high teacher–pupil ratios. The education ministry systematically denied petitions for classroom upgrades and building infrastructure. In the curriculum, Malay was a mandatory subject. Moreover, there were Malay language requirements for teaching certifications (Wu 2021). Schools did not have the option of choosing their own principals; often, the education ministry appointed a non-Chinese as a principal, although this restriction was relaxed after 1987 (Wu 2021). Likewise, proposals to create Chinese-medium schools – at both the secondary and tertiary levels – were also rejected (Liu 2015a). Exit options included enrolling in a private school or going abroad. Otherwise, loyalty (for about 30 percent of the population in 1983) meant attending a one-year Malay-medium transition school before proceeding to the Malay-language secondary school where Chinese was an optional subject (Kaplan and Baldauf 2003).

All this changed with the PH in power. English was again the language of science and math – much to the chagrin of the Malay nationalists. Mahathir even proposed bringing back English-medium schools. Moreover, in a big win for the Chinese minority, the government recognized the United Examinations Certificate (UEC), a standardized test used by independent Chinese language secondary schools. The shift did not manifest exclusively with languages of education. There were calls for non-Malays to take key ministerial positions; there were demands to reconsider the role of Islam; and there was the ratification of the International Convention on the Elimination of All Forms of Racial Discrimination (ICERD).

Since assuming office, the PN government has championed Malay interests. At the time of writing – in the midst of a pandemic – the jury is still out on where else we will see restrictions to Chinese accommodation. But for now, MCA is back in a ruling coalition, and the Chinese vernacular language remains a recognized language of the public schools at the primary level.

In sum, the Chinese minority in Malaysia share no ethnic identifier with the hegemon – whether language, religion, or phenotype. The absence of any crosscutting cleavage means it has not been possible for the Chinese to simply integrate with the Malays. And while there has been some episodic violence, historically the Malay-dominated government has adopted a position of ethnic accommodation rather than attempting to forcefully integrate the Chinese population.

Ethnic Malays in Singapore

In the aftermath of World War II, a group of ethnically diverse, English-educated men formed the PAP to pursue political independence for Singapore from the British colonial authority. Just as in Malaya, the British were willing to negotiate for Singapore's independence – with certain conditions. While communal tensions were likewise high in Singapore, the concern manifested more in terms of class – namely, communist ideology (Ong 2020). The communist threat was formidable in Singapore given the majority Chinese population, like it was in the other Straits Settlements. The ability of the supposed communists – closeted and championing under the guise of welfare economics – to protest, incite violence, and bring everything to halt on the island terrified the PAP and the British (Lee KC 1988; Lee KY 1998). Yet, the PAP and its leader Lee Kuan Yew (henceforth LKY) courted leftist leaders because the latter had the requisite electoral clout. Likewise, leftist leaders used the PAP as a cover to continue operation. The relationship was hostile. Both sides saw the other as an "albatross around the neck" (Lee KY 1998: 373).

To curry additional electoral support, the PAP "eagerly" recruited Malay activists in Singapore, including journalists, trade union leaders, and disgruntled Singapore Malay National Organization defectors (Rahim 2008). To this end, we see Malay accommodation on several important ethnic issues. First, the government signaled its willingness to recognize Malays as first among equals. While the special status was not explicitly stated as was the case in Malaya, the privilege afforded to the Malays manifested itself with language. Constitutionally, Malay was recognized as the singular national language: It is the language of the national anthem. And the recognition was not merely symbolic. The government spent considerable energy promoting the Malay language (The Sunday Times 1959b), legislating the compulsory learning of Malay in all schools – regardless of the medium of instruction (E. Tan 2007), and developing an Institute of Malayan Culture for popularizing and synthesizing Malayan culture (The Sunday Times, 1959a). In October 1961, education minister Yong Nyuk Lin opened the first Malay-language secondary school (Sang Nila Utama); in the first year, there were 447 students and 18 teachers (Gopinathan 1974). It was nothing short of "an attempt 'to cloak the infant state in the swaddling clothes of Malay-ness'" (Rahim 2008: 102).

The accommodation of the Malay minority would prove instrumental. In 1961 – after a public divorce between its original core and the leftist faction – the PAP made a political pivot. LKY and the British both recognized the PAP could not survive a perceived communist deluge – whether at the ballot box or on the streets (Lee KY 1998; Tan SS 2007). They believed that the only way to guarantee Singapore's independence from the British *and* to keep the island out of communist hands was to merge with Malaya to form Malaysia. For many reasons – particularly the addition of up to two million ethnic Chinese – the Tunku and the Alliance Party were not enthusiastic about a merger. To this end, what we see is the PAP committing to accommodate Malay demands – both domestically and externally. The PAP conceded to the ethnic Malays on matters of language, religion, and education. And, in fact, the concessions also included a number of political restrictions for Singapore's Chinese majority – including allocations of far fewer seats than its population size warranted and limitations on who could vote in (and contest) elections outside Singapore's immediate district (Ong 2020).

The merger was short-lived. Two years later, in 1965, the two entities went their separate ways. For the Malays in Singapore, the separation induced insecurity (Rahim 2008). The PAP did not help assuage the uncertainty. For the PAP, the ethnic Malays were no longer instrumental; they were neither essential allies against the communists nor pawns in a merger game. Instead, the government now saw the Malay minority as a potential political threat – with possible allegiance toward Kuala Lumpur rather than the PAP government. This perception shift was evident from the outset with census classification. Before separation, group identity was based on self-identification, specifically one's "native speech." An ethnic Chinese who spoke English or Malay at home need not explicitly identify as Chinese – as was the case for LKY who did not grow up speaking Chinese vernaculars (Lee KY 1998). However, after independence, "mother tongue" was autoidentified based on the "symbolic language of one's paternal ancestry" (E. Tan 2007: 79). Thus, an ethnic Chinese was Chinese even if they did not speak the language. Likewise, an ethnic Malay would always be Malay based on their parent's language, religion, and ancestry. And while there have been recent debates about who determines an individual's ethnicity – whether it is the individual, the relevant community, or a designated council (see Voltaire 2017) – what is substantively important here is that this racial categorization would institutionalize Malays as minorities (and, likewise, the Chinese as hegemons).

Despite the trepidation toward the Malay minority, the PAP chose – if not being outright resigned – to leave the ethnic status quo in place. This was certainly the case through the PAP First Generation Leadership. The de jure recognition of the Malays would remain unchanged. There was "no language issue" over the continued use of Malay as the national language (The Sunday Times 1966). Likewise, the lyrics to the national anthem were kept in Malay. Malay continued to be recognized as one of the four official languages. There were more than just Malay-medium schools; there were efforts to expand Malay education at the secondary level at well (Ibrahim 1999). Moreover, to encourage enrollment, there was exemption of full school fees (Li 1989). There are also Malay/Muslim community programs to assist individuals with education and training (e.g., Yayasan MENDAKI). Accommodation of the Malays was not limited to just language and education. Islam was also recognized – most substantively with the establishment of the Mosque Building Fund (Ibrahim 1999; Maricar 2016). It seemed that whatever the PAP did, it was "deliberate and conscious ... to recognize the special position of the Malays who are the indigenous people and who are in most need of assistance" – per the Singapore Constitution (Li 1989).

The PAP continued accommodating the Malays because it had other more pressing issues in the wake of the separation (Liu and Ricks 2012). First, there were economic challenges, including the lack of foreign reserves, insufficient land for growing rice, and skyrocketing unemployment. Next, there were also security concerns manifesting from Malaysia–Singapore tensions and the Malaysia–Indonesia *Konfrontasi* in Borneo. While Singapore was no longer part of Malaysia, there were still tensions with Jakarta (Lee KY 2000). And, third, racial riots in 1969 created concern for the government. This trifecta of challenges – a "systemic vulnerability" (Doner, Ritchie, and Slater 2005) – forced the PAP to "harp on the survival theme" (Chan and ul Haq 1987: 210) and relegate all other matters, including ethnic accommodation, to secondary importance (see Apfeld and Liu 2021).

On the one hand, the de jure accommodation has remained unchanged since independence. Indeed, there have been some grand overtures to the Malay minorities. For example, the introduction of group representation constituency (GRC) as an electoral system in 1988 built in a floor for minority parliamentary representation. GRCs required each slate of candidates to include at least one minority, thereby guaranteeing minority representation (Goh CT 1988). Likewise, the decision in 2016 to reserve the presidency for ethnic Malays enshrined their special status (Rodan 2018).

On the other hand, there has been a prevailing attitude among the Malay minority that the PAP was a "Chinese-based party whose multiracial ideology was little more than rhetoric" (Rahim 1998: 73). The de facto restrictions have highlighted Chinese privilege (Velyutham 2017). Consider recruitment into the armed forces and law enforcement services: The PAP doubted whether ethnic Malays would – or could – defend Singaporean interests in the event of an armed conflict with a neighboring Islamic state (Indonesia and Malaysia) or a domestic riot between the Chinese and Malays (Li 1989). This lack of trust meant Malays were systematically barred from the otherwise mandatory military service (Lee KY 2000) – thereby denying Malays the necessary expertise for future employment (Kassim 1974). And while the government lifted the conscription ban in 1973 – with full conscription happening in the 1980s (Ostwald 2014) – there were still limitations. Malays are not permitted in the navy or air force; likewise, they are not allowed to serve in key technological and leadership positions, such as the commando battalion, the armor battalion, and the naval diver unit (Hill and Lian 2013: 205–206).

The absence of Malays from prominent positions is not military specific. While there have always been ethnic Malays in the cabinet, their portfolios are systematically lower ranked. The highest-ranked Malay was Ahmad bin Ibrahim, who was the health minister (1960–1962) – a highly ranked portfolio at the time when the cabinet had only nine members. Later, there was Othman Wok, the singular Malay as the social affairs minister (1964–1977), followed by Ahmad Mattar (social affairs minister 1978–1984; environment minister 1985–1992). It was not until 2015 that we saw two ethnic Malays in the cabinet: Yaacob Ibrahim and Masagos Zulkifli (Chew and Liu 2020). Likewise, there have only been two Malays to ever serve as Supreme Court judges – neither being a chief justice (Supreme Court Singapore 2020). And when Malays are not absent, there are questions surrounding their merits versus their PAP party links. The GRC has made it difficult to ascertain whether the elected Malays got elected because of their own popularity or because of who else was on the ticket (E. Tan 2005). Likewise, in 2016 the government decided to reserve the upcoming presidential term for Malays – a decision that came hand-in-hand with a series of other criteria (i.e., restrictions). When the Presidential Elections Committee denied four other candidates' eligibility for the 2017 election, Halimah Yacob won in a noncontested race – an outcome Rodan (2018) argues was no different than a ceremonial appointment.

The tensions are also manifest in education. For example, the Malay Teachers Union proposed a national system of education where the Malay language stream would be given equal standing to English and Chinese. The proposal was rejected. Other grievances included the lack of facilities in the Malay-medium schools, the absence of high school certificate classes in the Malay track, and the proposed (Kassim 1974) – and eventual (Lee KY 2000) – shutting down of the Malay Studies Department at Nanyang

University. And finally, by the mid-1980s, with the transition from First Generation to Second, the PAP shut down all non-English schools (not just Malay but Chinese as well), citing declining enrollment numbers (Ganguly 2003; Gopinathan 1998). Since then, Malay has remained a subject of instruction.

Conclusion

This section examined ethnic politics when a minority shares no overlapping marker with the hegemon. Here, the government's only recourse – short of violence and repression – is to accommodate the minority. In both Malaysia and Singapore, accommodation has meant providing minority groups with linguistic recognition in public domains (e.g., schools), acknowledging religious differences, and recognizing the ancestral origins of the Malays. From a normative human rights standpoint, accommodation is preferred to violence.

Yet, de jure ethnic accommodation is not synonymous with de facto equality. This discrepancy is evident in how the Chinese in Malaysia and the Malays in Singapore both express their feelings as second-class citizens compared to their hegemon counterparts. In Malaysia, to solidify Malay dominance, the UMNO-led BN created a new ethnic category – *"bumiputera"* – that combined Malays with other indigenous groups. This move would increase the headcount of the hegemon Malays while minimizing the numerical presence of the Chinese, with subsequent brain-drain and out-migration implications (Ostwald and Oliver 2020; Ostwald and Subhan 2021). In Singapore, despite the adoption of multi-racial rhetoric, ethnic Malays often feel trivialized in the light of perceived Chinese privilege. Strategies in both countries have left the minorities feeling the accommodation has been nothing more than symbolic (Chew 2018; Velayutham 2017).

Nevertheless, accommodation persists. Here, it is important that we reemphasize that accommodation is one of two possible outcomes when ethnic boundaries are perceived as impermeable. Recall that how a hegemon treats a minority is the product of the political landscape during critical junctures. In Malaysia and Singapore, the most important critical juncture has been independence. In both cases, the hegemon needed minority support. In Malaysia, accommodating the Chinese was necessary for the British to grant independence. Likewise, in Singapore, recognizing the Malays was instrumental for fighting off the perceived communist aggression. In both cases, an external threat gave the minority group bargaining power that is far from guaranteed in ethnic power relations.

In the absence of such external threats, the hegemon has an alternative strategy for dealing with a minority: outright repression. We have extreme examples of this occurring in Southeast Asia – for example, the ethnic cleansing of the Chinese and Vietnamese minorities in Cambodia under the Khmer Rouge (Kiernan 2002) and the 2017 Rohingya crisis in Myanmar (Ware and Laoutides 2018). We also saw this in our discussion of the ethnic Chinese in Indonesia during Suharto's New Order government.

4 Ethnic Contention

In this section, we look at what happens when there is **contention**: *a relationship characterized by heightened mistrust by one group and (the possibility of) conflict*. Contention happens when (1) a minority chooses not to integrate; or (2) the hegemon that controls the state chooses not to accommodate the minority. When the minority and the hegemon share a commonality along one – and only one – cleavage, one of two scenarios is likely to manifest. In the first scenario, the government will attempt to integrate the minority along the one shared dimension. From the minority perspective, however, that singular marker is not sufficient for facilitating a common identity. Instead, the focus for the minority will be on one of the other two – if not both – ethnic markers where there is a distinction. In this scenario, when minorities reject integration efforts, the government will respond – often with repression and doubling down on the shared marker. As this becomes a cyclical process, the minority pushes back and mobilizes, electorally if not violently.

We see this play out with the ethnic Malays in Thailand's three southernmost provinces. Unlike the ethnic Lao and ethnic Chinese communities, ethnic Malays have engaged in more than a century of resistance to the Thai state's integration efforts. The insurgency has intensified over the past two decades, claiming more than 7,200 lives between 2004 and 2021. While some observers focus on the religious dimension of the struggle, the conflict is fundamentally about state efforts to integrate an ethnic minority against their will (International Crisis Group 2017). The Malay minority demands recognition and accommodation; conversely, the Thai state demands integration – if not outright assimilation (McCargo 2012; Streicher 2020).

Conversely, in the second scenario, it is the minority that believes the one shared ethnic marker is sufficient for integration. However, the hegemon's attention is on the two noncongruent markers. From their perspective, the minority is a distinct out-group. Overtures by the minority to integrate or blur the boundaries is seen as a (threat of) hostile takeover. The hegemon responds by hardening group boundaries – even if it means redefining the categories in

Table 6 One overlapping marker

	Ethnic Malays in Thailand (1909–)			Ethnic Chinese in Indonesia (1998–)	
	Minority	**Hegemon**		**Minority**	**Hegemon**
Language	Malay	Central Thai	*Language*	Indonesian	Indonesian
Religion	Islam	Buddhism	*Religion*	Buddhism/ Christianity/ Mixed	Islam
Phenotype	Phenotype 1	Phenotype 1	*Phenotype*	Phenotype 1	Phenotype 2

each ethnic marker and/or emphasizing new dimensions. As this is also – yet again – a cyclical process, the more the hegemon excludes the minority, the more the minority will attempt to integrate. And when fears of minority tyranny become heightened, the hegemon will respond with violence.

We see this dynamic unfold with the ethnic Chinese in Indonesia in the post-Suharto *reformasi* era. Unlike the integration experience of the Chinese minority in Thailand or the accommodation experience of the Chinese in Malaysia, the Chinese in Indonesia have endured repeated instances of ethnic contention – with the most brutal events in recent memory occurring in the aftermath of the 1997 Asian Financial Crisis. In May 1998, riots in Jakarta, Medan, Solo, and several other cities targeted the ethnic Chinese, resulting in more than 1,000 deaths, hundreds of rapes, and extensive property damage. While more than twenty years have passed since those events, violence and attacks on ethnic Chinese continue to mark the headlines. The "212 Movement" is an example – a mass protest demanding the arrest of then Jakarta Governor Basuki Tjahaja Purnama. As we will see in this section, although the ethnic Chinese have been part of the multiethnic Indonesian nation since independence and have integrated linguistically, they remain outsiders. **Table 6** summarizes these two cases.

Ethnic Malays in Thailand

In sharp contrast to the other two cases drawn from Thailand (see Section 2), the Malay minority in the three southern provinces of Narathiwat, Pattani, and Yala has not integrated well with the Thai identity. Indeed, conflict between the Malays and the Thais has been a recurring issue since 1909 when the Siamese state brought the Patani Sultanate – an area roughly coterminous with the three provinces – under direct control. Over the last two decades, violence in these three southernmost provinces has been common. From 2004 to 2021, violence between the Malay minority and the Thai state has resulted in more than 7,200 deaths, with fighting and attacks occurring periodically (although the attacks have diminished over the past three years).

The ethnic tone of the conflict is clearly evident: Advocates of Thai-ness have struggled – and failed – to turn the Malays into Thais (Selway 2007), while Malay insurgency organizations have advocated a form of ethnic nationalism based on a local identity tied to the historical Patani Sultanate (International Crisis Group 2017).[11] The Malay insurgency presents a threat to the state's nation-building efforts – efforts that include a state-approved Thai identity (McCargo 2008, 2012). Simply put, the Malay minority refuses to abandon its ethnic identity, while the hegemon Thais continue to coerce the Malays to be Thai.

The Patani Sultanate was incorporated into Siam through colonial mapping of the region – somewhat in parallel to the process that encapsulated the Lao northeast. Patani had paid tribute to Siamese kings on and off for centuries; the state's tributary status, however, also granted it substantial autonomy. As the British colonized the Malay peninsula in the late 1800s and early 1900s, the Siamese palace sought to secure suzerainty over the region. In 1909, the Siamese Palace and the British struck an agreement: Patani would remain under Siam, while the British would possess Kedah, Kelantan, and Terengganu (in present-day Malaysia).

The Siamese state soon began exercising more direct control over the Sultanate. This included administrative changes and efforts to Thai-ify the population. Similar to the Lao in the northeast, royal officials saw the south- erners as an inferior group that could be civilized through integration (Streicher 2020: 26–28). King Chulalongkorn, when planning for administrative reforms in Patani, suggested that the people should be encouraged – if not outright convinced – to "become Thai in both mind and manners" (quoted in Davisakd 2008: 78). Additionally, the region was divided along somewhat arbitrary provincial borders, spreading the Malay population across multiple administra- tive divisions.

Post absolute monarchy, the government of Field Marshall Phibulsongkram adopted a series of policies designed to unify Thai identity that were particularly cumbersome for the Malay people. They were referred to as "Southern Thais" or "Islamic Thais" to minimize their ethnic differences – again evidencing that Bangkok believed their identity could be integrated into the broader Thai-ness

---

[11] This is somewhat distinct from the Lao and Chinese groups whose traditional ethnic "home- lands" were located outside the Thai state boundaries. Selway (2021) has examined the impact of having a homeland within the state boundaries upon the Lanna people in northern Thailand.

(Thanet 2008: 105–108). The Malay language was forbidden – as were Malay fashions. There were also attempts to coerce the Muslims to abandon religious practices and to worship Buddhist icons instead (Wan Kadir 1987: 97–98). Over the ensuing years, efforts to force Malays to become Thai led to strong resentment toward Thai governance, wherein the Malays felt particularly pressured on linguistic and religious issues. These tensions resulted in local leaders issuing a formal demand in 1947 that Malays be free to practice their faith, use Islamic courts, be educated in Malay, use Malay in government offices, and be governed by a Muslim from the region. The Siamese state took these demands as a call for separatism, arresting local leaders for treason in early 1948 (Thanet 2008).

Tensions continued to build until the Dusun-Nyor incident on April 26–28, 1948, when at least 400 Malays and 30 police officers were killed (see Chaiwat 2007). Thousands of Malays fled across the border into Malaya; international attention turned to southern Thailand. The Phibun government suppressed the Malays, sentenced local leader Haji Sulong to prison, and continued its integration efforts. Haji Sulong would later disappear under mysterious circumstances after his release from prison – a disappearance the Malays took for state suppression (see Liow 2016: 124–126).

Continued contention led to the emergence of the *Barisan Revolusi Nasional* (National Revolutionary Movement: BRN) and the Patani United Liberation Organization (PULO) in the 1960s. Both organizations opposed the Thai state and its efforts to assimilate the Malays through the education system (Liow 2009). Antagonism increased with violent rebellion; the Thai state responded with force; and violence was then perpetrated by both the Malay organizations and the state through the 1970s.

In the late 1970s and early 1980s, the Thai state changed its approach to the region. It opted to combine suppression of the separatists with (1) an effort to win the "hearts and minds" of the people through development projects and (2) amnesty arrangements for some perpetrators of violence. The policy seemed relatively successful: Violence in the region decreased dramatically during the 1980s and 1990s. Despite this, relatively few ethnic Malays were represented in national political office. Moreover, many government bureaucrats still treated the Malay minority with derision (Ockey 2008: 144–149). Nevertheless, the 1990s provided some hope that a lasting peace could be achieved.

Things changed in 2001 when the Thaksin Shinawatra government (2000–2006) reformed the governance structures in southern Thailand. These reforms included an increase in extrajudicial disappearances (McCargo 2007). Thaksin supported the "War on Terror," backed the US invasion of Iraq, and sidelined ethnic Malays in parliament. When insurgents raided an army camp on January 4, 2004, Thaksin declared martial law in the south. In April that year, more than one hundred militants were killed – many of them as they hid within the historic Kru-Ze mosque. Tensions worsened in October, when seventy-eight protestors died in police custody in Tak Bai: They were crushed to death during transportation in police trucks.

Since 2004, violence has continued between the Malay insurgents, the Thai state, and people living in the three southernmost provinces. Despite some reports linking the violence with global Islamist movements, the Malay insurgents are primarily engaged in an ethnonationalist struggle rather than a global jihad (International Crisis Group 2017). The central challenge is the fight for recognition as a legitimate group within a state that endeavors to compel all Thai citizens to ascribe to a single, state-approved identity (McCargo 2012). We contend that this contentious relationship – in comparison to the integration of the Lao and the Chinese – can be interpreted through the contrasting perspectives adopted by the Malay minority and the hegemon Thais. To the Thai state, the recognition of a single shared marker suggests the Malays should integrate. To the ethnic Malays, however, the two unshared markers serve as a reminder of the need to remain separate. Put differently, the Thai state sees the ethnic boundary as porous while the Malays see it as fixed.

The one shared marker is phenotype. As discussed earlier, the hegemon advocated a Thai identity that included a broad spectrum of acceptable, sometimes genetically different phenotypes, including the people found along the Kra Isthmus and the Malay Peninsula, who exhibit somewhat darker skin pigmentation (Pongsakorn et al. 2013). The state refers to these people as Southern Thais (see Askew 2008). These people also share physical attributes with the Malay population, which has been reflected in genetic analysis that finds the two groups display "genetic homogeneity due to common biological ancestry" (Wibhu et al. 2014: 680). Put differently, Southern Thais and the people of Patani are essentially the same genetic population.

Aside from differences in apparel and the preference among some Malay men for facial hair, there are no definitive physically distinguishing characteristics that separate the ethnic Malays from the ethnic Thais in the south. Indeed, in a 1941 poster distributed in Songkhla province advocating dressing standards for proper "Thai Culture," there are two figures under the category of "inappropriate dress" who are clearly Muslim and wearing Muslim apparel (sarongs and a turban and a songkok). Conversely, in the next panel of "acceptable dress," the figures are in urban wear – suggesting that the Thai state imagined the bodies of these individuals to be Thai even though their clothing was not (see Winyu 2014: 14; also see Streicher 2020: 50–53). The hegemon, operating through the state, declared these people as Thai – a policy that continues today (see Anusorn

2019: 182–183). Phenotype, then, is one ethnic marker that is shared between the minority and the hegemon.

In contrast, religion provides a sharp division between the two communities. Wan Kadir Che Man (1987: 18–23), a native of the area, argues that religion in southern Thailand serves as the primary ethnic identifier for the Malays; it provides a unifying force that is fundamental to the Patani separatist movement. In his argument, the Islamic *ummah* (community) has played a central role in preserving the Malay identity against integration efforts by the Thai state. Indeed, before Patani was administratively integrated, Siamese officials linked Malay ethnic identity to Islam (Jory 2007: 258–259).

The distinction between the state-embraced Buddhism and Islam is stark, with both sides actively portraying the other as a potential threat to their religious practice. On the Thai side, Buddhism has become an integral element of the national identity. Alternative religions can be seen as aberrations; and since the early 2000s Islam has been popularly viewed as antithetical to Buddhism (McCargo 2012: chapter 2). For their part, ethnic Malays have long identified as Muslim – linking the religion to the mythic history of the Patani Sultanate (Liow 2016: 120–133). State efforts to manage Islam have alienated many Malays; it has spurred accusations that those collaborating with the government are betraying their religion (McCargo 2008: 49–51). The Thai state's attempts to integrate the Malays – for example, relabeling Malays as "Islamic Thais" – have been portrayed as oppressive and colonizing (Jory 2007). In short, religion is a vital cleavage that separates the Malay minority from the hegemon Thais.

It is important to note, though, that while religion is the primary cleavage, it alone is not sufficient to differentiate an identity. Other Muslim populations have been able to integrate within the Thai nation. For instance, the southern province of Satun – also bordering Malaysia, and where more than three-quarters of the population practices Islam – has been free of ethnic conflict. Ethnic Malay identity has diminished in the province, and most residents see themselves as Thai. As Parks (2009: 189–191) states, "The Muslim community in Satun seems to have lost its sense of Malay identity," instead identifying as "Thai Muslim." Muslim populations in Bangkok and other regions are also relatively well integrated into the Thai national identity (Liow 2009: 16; Van Roy 2016). In fact, Sonthi Boonyaratglin, former Commander of the Royal Thai Army who led the 2006 coup against Thaksin Shinawatra's government and then headed the military junta that ruled the country for two weeks, is Thai Muslim.

Here, we argue that our third ethnic marker – language – plays an important role in separating the two groups. The Thai state's efforts to teach Thai through-out the country included attempts to teach it among the Malays in the south. This was largely successful in Satun, where today almost the entire population speaks Thai (Parks 2009: 191–193). Conversely, the local Malay vernacular (Yawi) is a central component of the Malay identity in the former Patani Sultanate (Liow 2009: 17–18). Consider how PULO, in one of their documents in 1971, argued against Thai language education: "The Thai government is trying to teach the younger generation the Thai language and make them love the Thai government and respect the king so that in the future they will forget the Malay race and completely accept Thai nationality" (quoted in Suhrke 1977: 238). The struggle against learning Thai is tied to the endeavor to maintain Islamic education through the *pondok*, or Islamic schools. In short, these Islamic schools are important transmitters of religion *and* language – as well as resistance to the Thai state (Liow 2016: 114–116; McCargo 2008: 37–45).

The Thai state's lack of success in teaching Thai among the Malays separates the two groups. Wan Kadir (1987: 65–66) noted that at the time of his research, the language barrier segregated Malays and Thais. On the one hand, "the Malays villagers are too proud of their own cultural heritage to learn Thai." On the other hand, Thai government officials have resisted learning Malay. It does not help that the Thai government also refuses to recognize Malay as a working language. Instead, all official business must be conducted in Thai (see McCargo 2012: 80–81) – although the state has allowed for elementary education to be conducted in Malay in recent years. While Thai language capacity has spread since Wan Kadir conducted his research in the 1980s, there is still a barrier due to accent and fluency. Fluency in Thai stands as an important marker in "Thai-ness" – which often excludes the Malay minority (McCargo 2012: 124–125; also see Streicher 2020: 47–50). As such, interactions between the two groups are fraught with challenges.

One issue that our theory does not address, but which appears to play an important role in the Malay identity, is the influence of a commitment to the historical Patani Sultanate (Liow 2016). The ethnonational myth of the Patani nation having been colonized by the Thais spurs the conflict (Thanet 2008). Here, since our focus is on the costless markers of ethnic boundaries, our theory provides no clear guidance on this issue. Identifying a coethnic via belief in a shared homeland requires a degree of investment – rendering it a less effective mechanism to create identity in limited information settings (Chandra 2004). Furthermore, Chandra (2006) suggests that homeland myths should not serve as a defining characteristic of ethnic identity as they are not descent-based attributes – although they certainly can be used for mobilization (Selway 2021). In this case, the myth is embedded in and manifests in religion and language.

In sum, the only shared marker between the Malay minority and the Thai hegemon is phenotype. Based on this one overlap, the Thai state has endeavored to integrate rather than accommodate the Malays. On the one hand, the Thai government believes the ethnic Malays should be able to shape their identity to fit that proscribed by the state as "Thai Muslims." The Malay minority, on the other hand, see themselves as distinct – both in language and religion – and they aspire to maintain their distinctiveness. The contention, then, is fundamentally embedded in the conflict between integration and the desire to remain separate.

Ethnic Chinese in Indonesia

Indonesia houses incredible ethnic diversity. The census recognizes more than 1,300 ethnic groups (*suku bangsa*). The government considers most of these groups as *pribumi* – that is, "native Indonesians" – whose identities are tied to a geographic location in the archipelago. A few groups, however, are considered "foreign" (*asing*) no matter how many generations have lived in Indonesia. The largest of these "foreigners" is the Chinese community, making up about 1.2 percent of the country's total population in 2010. Indeed, the label non-*pribumi* almost always refers to the ethnic Chinese. Thus, discussions of the *pribumi* versus non-*pribumi* divide inevitably touch on markers of Chinese identity (Bertrand 2004; Setijadi 2019: 194–196). This ethnic boundary has long been a point of friction.

After independence (as discussed in our introductory section) group boundaries between the Chinese in Indonesia and the *pribumi* were impenetrable. The Chinese spoke a different language, (mostly) practiced a set of other faiths, and looked different. Sukarno recognized this and sought accommodation. His successor, Suharto, however, engaged in outright repression and forced assimilation. The Chinese had to abandon their cultural celebrations, language, and even their names to become Indonesian. The ethnic boundary went from one where there were no shared markers between the Chinese and *pribumi* to a situation where many Chinese adopted Indonesian as their first language[12] – making language a potential bridging identity marker. Here, we consider this period following Indonesia's most recent critical juncture – the end of Suharto's New Order in 1998 – where the Chinese minority and the *pribumi* hegemon share a single overlapping identity marker: language.

Over the past two decades, the Chinese minority has sought to better define their place within the broader Indonesian identity, including enhanced rights as

---

[12] The 2010 census indicates that less than one-quarter of ethnic Chinese still speak a Chinese vernacular at home regularly. In contrast, more than 60% speak Indonesian at home, with the remainder speaking local languages (e.g., Javanese and Malay). Contrast this to more than 92% of all Indonesians speaking Indonesian, with approximately 20% of them speaking it at home – thus making Indonesian the second-most common home language after Javanese.

citizens (Bertrand 2004; Dawis 2009). Ethnic Chinese politicians have emerged in relatively prominent positions, including Hasan Karman (former Singkawang Mayor), Christiandy Sanjaya (former West Kalimantan Deputy Governor), and the Tjahaja Purnama brothers: Basuki (former Jakarta Governor) and Basuri (former Belitung Regent). A record fifteen ethnic Chinese entered parliament in 2014. And while the number fell to eleven in 2019, that was also the same year that two parties headed by ethnic Chinese competed – albeit unsuccessfully – in parliamentary elections (Suryadinata 2019). Millennial and younger Chinese Indonesians, sometimes calling themselves *Chindos*, have taken to social media to proclaim their Indonesian-ness (Susilo and Sugihartati 2020). Attitudes have also shifted: Younger Chinese Indonesians want be accepted as Indonesians (Kuntjara and Hoon 2020). In short, the minority increasingly sees the ethnic boundary as penetrable.

To some extent, their efforts have been rewarded, as seen in the examples of political representation noted above. Moreover, there has been an increase in the activities of Chinese ethnicity-based social and professional organizations (Dawis 2009; Suryadinata 2019). Positive government actions have included officially removing the distinction between *pribumi* and non-*pribumi* (Presiden Republik Indonesia 1998); voiding legislation that banned public displays of Chinese culture and lifting the restrictions on Chinese language schools (President Republik Indonesia 1999); declaring Chinese New Year a national holiday (President Republik Indonesia 2002); and reducing the use of discriminatory terminology in government documents (President Republik Indonesia 2014). These acts are in stark contrast to the Suharto era (see Winarta 2008).

At the same time, segments among the *pribumi* hegemon have been unwilling to accept ethnically Chinese on equal grounds (Setijadi 2017a). This has resulted in recurring tensions and conflict, ranging from violent riots to mass protests to legal prosecutions. Prominently, Jakarta Governor Basuki Tjahaja Purnama's (BTP) 2016 reelection bid floundered due to rising anti-Chinese sentiments (Setijadi 2017b). BTP – better known by his Hakka Chinese nickname Ahok – is a Chinese Christian. He was the capital's first ethnic Chinese governor and only the second non-Muslim governor. He assumed the position when the previous governor (Joko Widodo) became president. Political opponents were uncomfortable with BTP's growing popularity. There was also increasing public frustration toward some of BTP's controversial policies, including forced evictions of the urban village communities and the Jakarta Cove land reclamation project (Setijadi 2017a). While campaigning for election in late September, BTP was caught on video claiming that some of his opponents were using a Qur'anic verse to discourage Muslims from voting for him. The video was edited with key omissions, making it appear like BTP said the

Qur'an itself was misleading the Muslims (Setijadi 2017b). Despite BTP's protests that the edits misrepresented his words, the video proved instrumental: He was found guilty in the court of public opinion.

Members of a hardline Islamist group accused BTP of violating the Blasphemy Law. A few days later, Indonesia's Council of Ulama (MUI) issued an edict pronouncing BTP's remarks "forbidden." The declaration gave the opposition the green light to protest the alleged blasphemy. The ensuing protests were some of the largest – if not the largest – ever seen in Indonesia. On November 4, upwards of 250,000 people gathered to demand BTP's conviction. The demonstration subsequently turned violent, with some protestors going into affluent ethnic Chinese neighborhoods and threatening to torch houses, evoking memories of 1998. Likewise, the demonstrators on December 2 numbered more than 500,000 (Peterson 2020; Steijadi 2019). Even after BTP was found guilty and sentenced to two years imprisonment – thereby ending his term as governor prematurely – protests continued, with calls for his execution.

BTP's double minority status made him an easy target. While the charges related to the Blasphemy Law were based on religion, BTP was often attacked for his Chinese ethnicity – with an "alarming" uptick in anti-Chinese hate speech (Setijadi 2017b: 3). In March 2016, retired General Prabowo Subianto – Suharto's son-in-law and a multi-occasion presidential candidate – issued a Facebook warning when he tagged BTP. He reminded "those friendly or affectionate with Chinese-Indonesians ... that they should not be arrogant with power or authority." The reminder also included a historical timeline referencing 1998 (Santoso 2016). In short, the BTP case heightened both religious and anti-Chinese intolerance.[13]

Other Chinese have also faced public attacks. As Setijadi (2019) chronicles, *pribumi* assaults on Chinese have included the 2007 "Alleyway 17" incident in Kalimantan, wherein rioters attacked a Chinese temple and properties over a traffic altercation; the 2016 Tanjung Balai riots against Chinese ethnics due to one woman's complaint about an overly loud call to prayer; and 2014 allegations that presidential candidate Joko Widodo might have Chinese ancestry. More recently, during the COVID-19 pandemic, politicians, social media, and traditional media have fueled anti-Chinese sentiments. Kompas TV even encouraged talk show panelists to state that COVID-19 was a Chinese biological weapon (Rakhmat 2020). This feeds into the persistent "narrative of the Chinese being outsiders who can never really belong in

---

[13] While Mietzer and Muhtadi (2019) find that anti-Chinese sentiments are still high, they have decreased in the aftermath of the BTP crisis. Likewise, Setijadi (2019) argues some of the anti-Chinese intolerance was less about the Chinese community per se and more about BTP as an individual.

Indonesia" – a sentiment that surveys have shown to remain strong (Setijadi 2017a: 11). Indeed, in one survey, most Indonesians did not feel comfortable with a Chinese Indonesian in political leadership (Fossati, Hui, and Negara 2017). Likewise, another survey experiment found that for the Muslim majority, religious difference is of lesser importance than Chinese ethnicity per se when it comes to out-group tolerance (Sumaktoyo 2021).

Our theoretical predictions, then, align with this case. The Chinese minority and the *pribumi* hegemon are distinct in both religion and phenotype; but, thanks to Suharto's assimilation policies, the two groups share a language. The minority Chinese have taken their three-decade-long brutal New Order integration – including their adoption of the national tongue – as sufficient cause for recognition as Indonesians. They have claimed – and are still claiming – their rights as citizens of the country. At the same time, elements of the *pribumi* population focus on their religious differences. Whether Buddhism, Confucianism, or Christianity, religion has been used to politically define the Chinese (Suryadinata 2005). Likewise, calling attention to appearance means the Chinese are eternally defined as *asing* – that is, foreign. The conflicting expectations increase the odds of minority persecution. As long as the Chinese are seen as Chinese and not Indonesian – whether it is because of religion or because of phenotype – there remains the potential for violence.

Conclusion

This section highlighted how a shared single ethnic marker – whether it is phenotype (e.g., Malays in Thailand) or language (e.g., Chinese in Indonesia) – can foster as many challenges as it resolves. For one group, the shared marker is seen as a justification for why the minority should not be considered a minority. In other words, the group believes that the minority should receive no special recognition for their distinctiveness but should be recognized within the larger national identity. This belief can be present among those in the minority or the hegemon. Conversely, for the other group, the two distinct markers maintain the minority as separate. They foster a sufficiently impenetrable boundary between ethnicities whereby either the minority is unwilling to abandon their identity to integrate or the hegemon is afraid of the minority merging and tyrannizing from within. In Thailand, the separation manifested in the form of an ethnonationalist movement based on language and religion. In Indonesia, the *pribumi* hegemon maintains that the Chinese minority are distinct through religious and pheno-typical markers. In both cases, contention between the minority's distinction pitted against the hegemon has resulted in outbreaks of violence – albeit in different forms.

These differences are instructive. In Thailand, part of the minority has embraced violent rebellion. The ethnonationalist movement sees Patani as its historic homeland while the Thais are invader and colonizers. In Indonesia, the Chinese minority has been subject to repeated attacks by *pribumi* mobs due to fits of economic jealousy, anti-communism, and ethnonationalist surges. The *pribumi* see the Chinese as outsiders. The indigeneity of a community, then, plays a role in violence type. That said, our theory does not differentiate between *which* conflict types are more likely to occur. Instead, it merely predicts the *whether* – namely, conflict is more likely to occur where only a single ethnic marker overlaps between groups. Our theory also does not account for *when* the conflicts are more likely to occur. While tensions in southern Thailand have been ongoing for more than a century, the fighting itself has ebbed and flowed. Likewise, violence against the Chinese in Indonesia is intermittent.

5 Conclusion

As the annual rainy season approaches, rural ethnic Lao communities on both sides of the Mekong prepare for the tradition of *bun bang fai* (rocket festival). Participants assemble homemade rockets that they launch into the air, celebrating the coming planting season, and – depending on the local legend – ushering in the rains. The rocket-makers also compete for social prestige and cash depending on the rocket's performance. The most famous competition is a three-day event in Yasothon province in northeastern Thailand. The Tourism Authority of Thailand (TAT) promotes this annual festival as a celebration of Thai culture. And, more importantly for our purposes, it is a festival promoting a history in Thailand – one that is described in TAT materials in English and Thai sans reference to its Lao origins.[14] *Bun bang fai* is not a Lao tradition but rather an "Isan," "Northeastern" tradition. In essence, it is "Thai."

Such integration is possible because of cross-cutting ethnic markers that have allowed ethnic Lao and ethnic Thais to see themselves as part of the same Thai identity. We demonstrated in the preceding sections how the interaction and overlap of ethnic markers allow for some groups to integrate, while others are accommodated, and still others develop into contention.

The central point here is about ethnic boundaries and the degree to which they can become porous. When both the minority and the hegemon see boundaries as permeable – thanks to multiple overlapping ethnic markers – integration is possible. Conversely, when both groups perceive borders to be fixed,

---

[14] While TAT frequently updates its website, versions of its Yasothon page include descriptions of the "Isan" or "Northeastern" character of the *bun bang fai* festival. Examples include the 2005 (https://tinyurl.com/skft24cu) and 2018 (https://tinyurl.com/3xwx5j8h) press releases for the festival (accessed March 18, 2021).

accommodation is the only acceptable option (assuming the hegemon does not outright repress the minority). And finally, when the two groups have incompatible expectations about their boundaries, we see contention. This occurs when one group – usually the hegemon, but not always – observes a shared marker and thus decides to focus on integration; meanwhile, the other group – often the minority, but again, not always – sees its boundaries as fixed and thus integration is not possible. Of course, these are theoretical ideal types. We argue that the permeability of ethnic boundaries – as determined by overlapping markers – affects the probability of ethnic integration, accommodation, and contentious outcomes.

Additionally, we contend that the emerging outcome is often in equilibrium until there is a critical juncture. Critical junctures are shifts in the political landscape; they are often opportunities for the hegemon to reconsider its relationship with the minority. In the absence of these shifts, there is a strong bias toward the status quo.

The application of this interpretation of ethnicity and politics across our six cases provides some leverage to understand how ethnic groups interact in Southeast Asia. **Table 3** outlined these comparisons in the way we presented them in the text. At this point, though, we can gain even more insight through two alternative perspectives. First, we have considered three ethnic groups in Thailand: two have integrated while a third experiences contention. This within-country variation allows us to see a spectrum of outcomes, with integration being perhaps most successful among the Lao minority. The Chinese minority has also integrated, although they retain some distinctiveness – especially in recent decades as interaction with other Chinese communities outside of Thailand has become easier. Both ethnic minorities, however, have largely adopted a Thai identity. This was possible thanks to their overlapping markers of religion and phenotype. Conversely, the Malay minority concentrated in Thailand's three southernmost provinces has resisted integration efforts. This is due to the mismatch in perceptions between the state, which believes the minority should integrate, and the Malay minority, who perceives an impermeable ethnic boundary based upon language and religion. Interestingly, we noted that Thai Muslims in nearby Satun province have integrated, despite their religious differences from the hegemon. This integration was successful in large part due to their adoption of the Thai language (and, thus, the Muslims in Satun share two markers with the politically dominant Thais).

This within-country comparison allows us to see how multiple overlapping markers of ethnicity created a porous boundary for the Lao, the Chinese, and even the Malays in Satun. Conversely, the continued persistence of a fixed boundary between the ethnic Malays in Narathiwat, Yala, and Pattani and the hegemon Thais is based largely upon the Malay group's capacity to maintain a linguistic and religious barrier between themselves and the Thai government. The Thai government, for their part, believes that the Malays should integrate rather than be accommodated. Under such conditions, contention persists.

Second, we have discussed three ethnic Chinese communities across the region in Thailand, Malaysia, and Indonesia. As noted earlier, in Thailand the ethnic boundary became porous due to intermarriage between the Chinese minority and the Thai hegemon that reduced phenotypical differences. Beyond this, the Thai elites, many of whom were *lukjin*, the product of this intermingling, adopted a flexible understanding of the Thai phenotype. The soft boundaries between Chinese and Thai religious practices also blurred group identities. Thus, the Chinese minority could – and did – become Thai, which has been further facilitated by widespread use of the Thai language among ethnic Chinese despite retaining Chinese for in-group interaction. Alternatively, the Chinese community in Malaysia shares no markers with the Malay hegemon. The lack of overlap on any marker has left both sides unwilling to attempt integration. This has led to a general policy of accommodation, albeit one that de facto disadvantages the Chinese. The Indonesian case points to a situation wherein many among the ethnic Chinese have adopted the Indonesian language. And while this serves as an overlapping marker with the hegemon, in the absence of any other overlapping markers – something the *pribumi* population has periodically labored to maintain – the two communities continue to struggle to find an appropriate policy. This, in turn, has been the fodder for sporadic violence.

This multicountry comparison of the treatment of a single ethnic group also demonstrates the explanatory power of the theory. In all three cases, the ethnic Chinese are a minority that is not considered native. Yet, in one case they have been able to successfully integrate thanks to porous ethnic boundaries because of overlapping markers. In another, they have been accommodated. But in the third, we see contention. This suggests that how a state engages with an ethnic group is not driven by the group itself – that is, it is not because the group is Chinese per se or because the group is of immigrant origins. Instead, it is because of the degree to which ethnic boundaries with the hegemon can be crossed.

As evidence, consider that we also presented the ethnic Malay as minorities in two cases: Singapore and Thailand. In the Singapore case, the ethnic Malay are accommodated. While there are de facto shortcomings, from a de jure standpoint the Malay are afforded special recognition – whether it is in language use or religious practices. Conversely, as we established earlier, the situation between the ethnic Malay and the Thai state has been marked by violence. Taken altogether, this also suggests that when we do see conflicts, they are not the result of some civilizational clash.

The contribution of this Element, then, is to turn our focus toward the composite nature of ethnic identity. We do so by disaggregating the different markers of identity. And while we have focused on the "costless" signals of language, religion, and phenotype, they are certainly not the only ethnic markers (Chandra 2004). Ethnicity can include tribes, nationalities, and castes. It can also include geographical historical origins – like what we saw in southern Thailand with the Malays and the Patani Sultanate. And while it may not be a descent-based attribute (see Chandra 2006), it is a marker that can be politicized as rigid and fixed (Liu and Selway 2021).

By disaggregating the different ethnic markers, we are able to examine the degree to which they create a permeable or flexible boundary between ethnic groups. In a region as diverse as Southeast Asia, the social and political borders created between ethnic groups can have seismic implications for the capacity of millions of people to interact. Also, as we recognize that ethnic boundaries are sociopolitical constructs, it is imperative to better understand the ways in which such boundaries can either be made permeable or, when that is not possible, how accommodations can be made to reduce the propensity for ethnic conflict.

References

Abdelal, Rawi, Yoshiko M. Herrera, Alastair Iain Johnston, and Rose McDermott. 2009. *Measuring Identity: A Guide for Social Scientists*. New York: Cambridge University Press.

Abdul Samad, Paridah. 1998. *Tun Abdul Razak: A Phenomenon in Malaysian Politics*. Kuala Lumpur: Affluent Master Sdn. Bhd.

Abdullah, Walid Jumblatt. 2016. "Managing minorities in competitive authoritarian states: Multiracialism and the hijab issue in Singapore." *Indonesia and the Malay World* 44(129):211–228.

Abdullah, Walid Jumblatt. 2019. "The Mahathir effect in Malaysia's 2018 election: The role of credible personalities in regime transitions." *Democratization* 26(3):521–536.

Abinales, Patricio N. 2000. *Making Mindanao: Cotabato and Davao in the Formation of the Philippine Nation-state*. Manila: Ateneo University Press.

Ali, Syed Husin. 2008. *The Malays: Their Problems and Future*. Petaling Jaya, Malaysia: The Other Press.

Aliran. 2019. "Competing narratives and managing diversity in 'New Malaysia.'" (May 22, 2019). https://aliran.com/thinking-allowed-online/competing-narratives-and-managing-diversity-in-new-malaysia/ (accessed April 12, 2021).

Amrith, Sunil S. 2011. *Migration and Diaspora in Modern Asia*. New York: Cambridge University Press.

Ananta, Aris, Evi Nurvidya Arifin, and Bakhtiar Kusnadi. 2008. "Chinese Indonesians in Indonesia and the Province of Riau Archipelago: A demographic analysis." pp. 17–47 in *Ethnic Chinese in Contemporary Indonesia*, edited by Leo Suryadinata. Singapore: Chinese Heritage Centre and ISEAS.

Andaya, Barbara Watson, and Leonard Y. Andaya. 2017. *A History of Malaysia*. London: Palgrave.

Anderson, Benedict. 2006. *Language and Power: Exploring Political Cultures in Indonesia*. Singapore: Equinox Publishing (Asia) Pte Ltd.

Anusorn Unno. 2019. *We Love Mr King: Malay Muslims of Southern Thailand in the Wake of the Unrest*. Singapore: ISEAS Press.

Apfeld, Brendan, and Amy H. Liu. 2021. "Education prioritization and language spread." *Social Science Journal* 58(3):366–382.

Askew, Marc. 2008. *Performing Political Identity: The Democrat Party in Southern Thailand*. Chiang Mai: Silkworm Books.

Aspinall, Edward. 2009. *Islam and the Nation: Separatist Rebellion in Aceh, Indonesia*. Stanford, CA: Stanford University Press.

Aspinall, Edward. 2011. "Democratization and ethnic politics in Indonesia: Nine theses." *Journal of East Asian Studies* 11(2):289–319.

Aymonier, Etienne. 2000. *Isan Travels: Northeast Thailand's Economy in 1883–1884* (Walter E. J. Tips, trans.). Bangkok: White Lotus Press. (Original work published as *Voyage dans le Laos,* 2 Volumes, 1895, 1897).

Barr, Michael D., and Zlatko Skrbiš. 2008. *Constructing Singapore: Elitism, Ethnicity and the Nation-building Project*. Copenhagen: Nias Press.

Barter, Shane J. 2020. *Fighting Armed Conflict in Southeast Asia*. New York: Cambridge University Press.

Barth, Fredrik. 1969. *Ethnic Groups and Boundaries*. Long Grove, IL: Waveland Press.

Bertrand, Jacques. 2004. *Nationalism and Ethnic Conflict in Indonesia*. New York: Cambridge University Press.

Boonsanong Punyodyana. 1971. *Chinese-Thai Differential Assimilation in Bangkok: An Exploratory Study*. Southeast Asia Data paper no. 79. Ithaca, NY: Cornell University Press.

Bowie, Katherine A. 2014. "Of Buddhism and militarism in Northern Thailand: Solving the puzzle of the Saint Khruubaa Srivichai." *Journal of Asian Studies* 73(3):711–732.

Breazeale, Kennon. 1975. *The integration of the Lao States into the Thai kingdom*. PhD dissertation. University of Oxford, St. Anthony's College.

Bun, Chan Kwok and Tong Chee Kiong. 1993. "Rethinking assimilation and ethnicity: The Chinese in Thailand." *The International Migration Review* 27(1):140–168.

Burhanudeen, Hafriza. 2006. *Language and social behavior: Voices from the Malay world*. PhD dissertation in Political Science. Bangi, Malaysia: Universiti Kebangsaan Malaysia.

Callahan, William A. 2003. "Beyond cosmopolitanism and nationalism: Diasporic Chinese and neo-nationalism in China and Thailand." *International Organization* 57(3):481–517.

Case, William. 1991. "Comparative Malaysian leadership: Tunku Abdul Rahman and Mahathir Mohamad." *Asian Survey* 31(5):456–473.

Cederman, Lars-Erik, Brian Min, and Andreas Wimmer. 2010. "Ethnic Power Relations dataset." Harvard Dataverse. https://doi.org/10.7910/DVN/NDJUJM.

Central Intelligence Agency. 2020. *The World Factbook*. Washington DC: Central Intelligence Agency.

Chaiwat Satha-Anand. 2007. "The silence of the bullet monument: Violence and "truth" management, Dusun-nyor 1948, and Kru-Ze 2004." pp 11–34 in *Rethinking Thailand's Southern Violence*, edited by Duncan McCargo. Singapore: NUS Press.

Chan, Heng Chee, and Obaid ul Haq (Eds.). 1987. *The Prophetic and the Political: Selected Speeches and Writings of S. Rajaratnam*. Singapore: Graham Brash Pte Ltd.

Chandra, Kanchan. 2004. *Why Ethnic Parties Succeed: Patronage and Ethnic Head Counts in India*. New York: Cambridge University Press.

Chandra, Kanchan. 2006. "What is ethnic identity and does it matter?" *Annual Review of Political Science* 9:397–424.

Chandra, Kanchan, and Steven Wilkinson. 2008. "Measuring the effect of 'ethnicity.'" *Comparative Political Studies* 41(4–5):515–563.

Chaun Phongphichit. 2010. *Lukjin rak chat* [Chinese Descendants Love the Nation]. Bangkok: Matichon Press.

Chauvel, Richard. 2005. *Constructing Papuan Nationalism: History, Ethnicity, and Adaptation*. Policy Studies no. 14. Washington, DC: East-West Center.

Chew, Keith Padraic and Amy H. Liu. 2020. "Ethnicity, gender, and intersectionality in government cabinets: Evidence from Southeast Asia." Working Paper.

Chew, Peter K. H. 2018. "Racism in Singapore: A review and recommendations for future research." *Journal of Pacific Rim Psychology* 12, E5. https://doi .org/10.1017/prp.2018.3.

Chin, Peng. 2004. *Dialogues with Chin Peng: New Light on the Malayan Communist Party*. Singapore: National University of Singapore Press.

China Qiaowang. 2018. "大马华社乐见林冠英任财政部长 望稳定马币汇率" [Malaysian Chinese Society welcomes Lim Guan Eng as finance minister, and hopes to stabilize the ringgit exchange rate"] (May 15, 2018). www .chinaqw.com/hqhr/2018/05-15/189755.shtml (accessed April 12, 2021).

Chua, Beng-Huat, and Eddie Kuo. 1998. "The making of a new nation: Cultural construction and national identity in Singapore." pp. 35–68 in *From Beijing to Port Moresby: The Politics of National Identity in Cultural Policies*, edited by Virginia Domingues and David Wu. Amsterdam: Gordon and Breach.

Coppel, Charles A. 1997. "Revisiting Furnivall's 'plural society': Colonial Java as a mestizo society?" *Ethnic and Racial Studies* 20(3):562–579.

Cribb, Robert, and Charles A. Coppel. 2009. "A genocide that never was: Explaining the myth of anti-Chinese massacres in Indonesia, 1965–66." *Journal of Genocide Research* 11(4):447–465.

Csata, Zsombor, Roman Hlatky, and Amy H. Liu. 2021. "How to head count ethnic minorities: Validity of census surveys versus other identification strategies." *East European Politics* 37(3):572–592.

Davidson, Jamie S. 2008a. *From Rebellion to Riots: Collective Violence in Indonesian Borneo*. Madison: University of Wisconsin Press.

Davidson, Jamie S. 2008b. "The study of political ethnicity in Southeast Asia." pp. 199–226 in *Southeast Asia in Political Science: Theory, Region, and Qualitative Analysis*, edited by Erik Kuhonta, Dan Slater, and Tuong Vu. Stanford, CA: Stanford University Press.

Davisakd Puaksom. 2008. "Of a lesser brilliance: Patani historiography in contention." pp 71–88 in *Thai South and Malay North: Ethnic Interactions on a Plural Penninsula*, edited by Michael J. Montesano and Patrick Jory. Singapore: NUS Press.

Dawis, Aimee. 2009. *The Chinese of Indonesia and Their Search for Identity*. Amherst, NY: Cambria Press.

Diller, Anthony. 2002. "What makes Central Thai a national language?" pp 71–107 in *National Identity and its Defenders: Thailand Today*, edited by Craig J. Reynolds. Chiang Mai: Silkworm Books.

Doner, Richard F., Bryan K. Ritchie, and Dan Slater. 2005. "Systemic vulnerability and the origins of developmental states." *International Organization* 59(2):327–361.

Draper, John, and Peerasit Kamnuansilpa. 2018. "The Thai Lao question: The reappearance of Thailand's ethnic Lao community and related polity questions." *Asian Ethnicity* 19(1):81–105.

Draper, John, and Joel Sawat Selway. 2019. "A new dataset on horizontal structural ethnic inequalities in Thailand in order to address Sustainable Development Goal 10." *Social Indicators Research* 141(1):275–297.

The Economist. 2020. "Indonesia's government wants to get on with China in private: While Pandering to anti-Chinese sentiment domestically." (February 13, 2020). www.economist.com/asia/2020/02/13/indonesias-government-wants-to-get-on-with-china-in-private (accessed April 10, 2021).

Enfield, N. J. 2002. "How to define 'Lao', 'Thai', and 'Isan' language? A view from linguistic science. *Tai Culture* 7(1):62–67.

Esman, Milton J. 1987. "Ethnic politics and economic power." *Comparative Politics* 19(4):395–418.

Fossati, Diego, Hui Yew-Foong, and Siwage Dharma Negara. 2017. "The Indonesia National Survey Project: Economy, society, and politics." *ISEAS Trends in Southeast Asia*, No. 10.

Fox, Colm. 2018. "Candidate-centric systems and the politicization of ethnicity: Evidence from Indonesia." *Democratization* 25(7):1190–1209.

Fox, Jonathan. 2008. *A World Survey of Religion and the State*. New York: Cambridge University Press.

Ganguly, Šumit. 2003. "The politics of language policies in Malaysia and Singapore." pp. 239–262 in *Fighting Words: Language Policy and Ethnic Relations in Asia*, edited by Michael E. Brown and Šumit Ganguly. Cambridge, MA: The MIT Press.

Goh, Chok Tong. 1988. *Singapore Parliamentary Debates, Official Report* 50(180): January 11, 1988.

Gopinathan, Saravanan. 1974. *Towards a National System of Education in Singapore 1945–1973*. Singapore: Oxford University Press.

Gopinathan, Saravanan. 1998. "Language policy changes 1979–1997: Politics and pedagogy." pp. 19–44 in *Language, Society and Education in Singapore: Issues and Trends*, edited by S. Gopinathan, Anne Pakir, Wah Kam Ho, and Vanithamani Saravanan. Singapore: Times Academic Press.

Grabowsky, Volker. 1996. "The Thai census of 1904: Translation and analysis." *Journal of the Siam Society* 84(1):49–86.

Hamilton, A. W. 1924. "Chinese loan-words in Malay." *Journal of the Malayan Branch of the Royal Asiatic Society* 2(1):48–56.

Harish, S. P. 2006. "Ethnic or religious cleavage? Investigating the nature of the conflict in southern Thailand." *Contemporary Southeast Asia* 28(1):48–69.

Heng, Pek Koon. 1988. *Chinese Politics in Malaysia: A History of the Malaysian Chinese Association*. Oxford: Oxford University Press.

Hill, Ann Maxwell. 1992. "Chinese funerals and Chinese ethnicity in Chiang Mai, Thailand." *Ethnology* 31(4):315–330.

Hill, Michael, and Kwen Fee Lian. 2013. *The Politics of Nation Building and Citizenship in Singapore*. Abingdon: Routledge.

Hirschman, Charles. 1986. "The making of race in Colonial Malaya: Political economy and racial ideology." *Sociological Forum* 1(2):330–361.

Horowitz, Donald L. 1971. "Three dimensions of ethnic politics." *World Politics* 23(2):232–244.

Horowitz, Donald L. 1985. *Ethnic Groups in Conflict*. Berkeley: University of California Press.

Hu, Fu, and Yun-han Chu. 2020. *Asian Barometer: All Rounds*. Taipei: National Taiwan University.

Human Rights Watch. 1998. "Indonesia alert: Economic crisis leads to scapegoating of ethnic Chinese, February 1998." (February 18). www.hrw.org/report/1998/02/18/indonesia-alert/economic-crisis-leads-scapegoating-ethnic-chinese-february-1998# (accessed April 12, 2021).

Ibrahim, Faisal, Norhayati Manaf, Thong Lai, et al. 2010. "Re-visiting Malay stereotypes: A case study among Malaysian and Indonesian Chinese students." *SEGi Review* 3(2):153–163.

Ibrahim, Zuraidah. 1999. "The Malay mobilisers: Ahmad Ibrahim, Othman Wok, Yaacob Mohamed, and Rahim Ishak." pp. 117–130 in *Lee's Lieutenants: Singapore's Old Guard*, edited by Peng Er Lam and Kevin Y. L. Tan. St. Leonards: Allen & Unwin.

Iijima, Akiko. 2018. "The invention of "Isan" history." *Journal of the Siam Society* 106:171–199.

International Crisis Group. 2017. "Jihadism in Southern Thailand: A phantom menace." Asia Report No. 291. Brussels: International Crisis Group.

Jory, Patrick. 2007. "From *Melayu Patani* to Thai Muslim: The spectre of ethnic identity in southern Thailand." *South East Asian Research* 15(2):255–279.

Kamala Tiyavanich. 1997. *Forest Recollections: Wandering Monks in Twentieth-Century Thailand*. Honolulu: University of Hawai'i Press.

Kaplan, Robert B., and Richard B. Baldauf Jr., 2003. *Language and Language-in-Education Planning in the Pacific Basin*. Dordrecht: Kluwer Academic Publishers.

Kasian Tejapira. 2009. "The misbehaving *jeks*: The evolving regime of Thainess and Sino-Thai challenges." *Asian Ethnicity* 10(3):263–283.

Kassim, Ismail. 1974. *Problems of Elite Cohesion: A Perspective from a Minority Community*. Singapore: Singapore University Press.

Kaufman, Stuart J. 2011. "Symbols, frames, and violence: Studying ethnic war in the Philippines." *International Studies Quarterly* 55(4):937–958.

Kaufman, Stuart J. 2013. "The limits of nation-building in the Philippines." *International Area Studies Review* 16(1):3–23.

Keyes, Charles F. 1967. *Isan Regionalism in Northeastern Thailand*. Ithaca, NY: Cornell University Press.

Keyes, Charles F. 1997. "Cultural diversity and national identity in Thailand." pp. 197–231 in *Government Policies and Ethnic Relations in Asia and the Pacific*, edited by Michael E. Brown and Sumit Ganguly. Cambridge, MA: MIT Press.

Keyes, Charles F. 2003. "The politics of language in Thailand and Laos." pp. 177–210 in *Fighting Words: Language Policy and Ethnic Relations in Asia*, edited by. Michael E. Brown and Sumit Ganguly. Cambridge, MA: MIT Press.

Keyes, Charles F. 2014. *Finding their Voice: Northeastern Villagers and the Thai State*. Chiang Mai: Silkworm Books.

Khong, Kim Hoong. 1991. "Malaysia's general election 1990: continuity, change, and ethnic politics." Research Notes and Discussions Paper No. 74. Singapore: Institute of Southeast Asian Studies.

Kiernan, Ben. 2002. *The Pol Pot Regime: Race, Power, and Genocide in Cambodia under the Khmer Rouge, 1975–1979*. New Haven, CT: Yale University Press.

Kim, Diana S. 2020. *Empires of Vice: The Rise of Opium Prohibition Across Southeast Asia*. Princeton, NJ: Princeton University Press.

Kobkua Suwannathat-pian. 1995. *Thailand's Durable Premier: Phibul Through Three Decades, 1932–1957*. Kuala Lumpur: Oxford University Press.

Kong, Lily, and Brenda S. A. Yeoh. 1997. "The construction of national identity through the production of ritual and spectacle: An analysis of National Day parades in Singapore." *Political Geography* 16(3):213–239.

Kuntjara, Esther, and Chang-Yau Hoon. 2020. "Reassessing Chinese Indonesian stereotypes: Two decades after *Reformasi*." *South East Asia Research* 28(2): 199–216.

Labini, Paulo Sylos. 2001. *Underdevelopment: A Strategy for Reform*. Cambridge: Cambridge University Press.

Lee, Hock Guan. 2007. "Ethnic politics, national development and language policy in Malaysia." pp. 118–150 in *Language, Nation and Development in Southeast Asia*, edited by Hock Guan Lee and Leo Suryadinata. Singapore: ISEAS.

Lee, Hugo Yu-Hsiu. 2014. "Losing Chinese as the first language in Thailand." *Asian Social Science* 10(6):176–193.

Lee, Khoon Choy. 1988. *On the Beat to the Hustings*. Singapore: Times Centre.

Lee, Kuan Yew. 1998. *The Singapore Story: Memoirs of Lee Kuan Yew*. Singapore: Prentice Hall.

Lee, Kuan Yew. 2000. *From Third World to First: The Singapore Story*. Singapore: Times Media Private Limited.

Leong, Trinna. 2018. "Malaysia appoints first Chinese finance minister in 44 years." *The Strait Times* (May 13, 2018). www.straitstimes.com/asia/se-asia/malaysia-appoints-first-chinese-finance-minister-in-44-years (accessed April 12, 2021).

Leow, Rachel. 2016. *Taming Babel: Language in the Making of Malaysia*. Cambridge: Cambridge University Press.

Lewis, Paul M., Gary F. Simons, and Charles D. Fennig (Eds.). 2016. *Ethnologue: Languages of the World*. Dallas: SIL International.

Li, Tania. 1989. *Malays in Singapore: Culture, Economy, and Ideology*. Singapore: Oxford University Press.

Lieberman, Evan S., and Prerna Singh. 2017. "Census enumeration and group conflict: A global analysis of the consequences of counting." *World Politics* 69(1):1–53.

Liow, Joseph Chinyong. 2009. *Islam, Education and Reform in Southern Thailand: Tradition and Transformation*. Singapore: ISEAS Press.

Liow, Joseph Chinyong. 2016. *Religion and Nationalism in Southeast Asia*. Cambridge: Cambridge University Press.

Liu, Amy H. 2015a. *Standardizing Diversity: The Political Economy of Language Regimes*. Philadelphia: University of Pennsylvania Press.

Liu, Amy H. 2015b. "The politics of language regime: A comparative analysis of Southeast Asia." pp. 137–153 in *State Traditions and Language Regimes*, edited by Linda Cardinal and Selma K. Sonntag. Montreal: McGill-Queen's Press.

Liu, Amy H. 2021. *The Language of Political Incorporation*: Chinese Migrants in Europe. Philadelphia: Temple University Press.

Liu, Amy H., and Elise Pizzi. 2018. "Language of economic growth: A new measure of linguistic heterogeneity." *British Journal of Political Science* 48(4):953–980.

Liu, Amy H., and Jacob I. Ricks. 2012. "Coalitions and language politics: Policy shifts in southeast Asia." *World Politics* 64(3):476–506.

Liu, Amy H, and Joel Sawat Selway. 2021. "Explaining identity formation in Asia." *Asian Politics & Policy* 13(1):6–17.

Maricar, Abdul Razak Hassan. 2016. "The Islamic religious council of Singapore (MUIS) journey: Continuing the pursuit of excellence – legacy from the past." pp. 273–279 in *MAJULAH! 50 Years of Malay/Muslim Community in Singapore*, edited by Zainul Abidin Rasheed and Norshahril Saat. Singapore: World Scientific.

May, R. J. 2003. "Ethnicity in the Philippines." pp. 136–156 in *Ethnicity in Asia*, edited by Colin Mackerras. London: Routledge.

MCA. 2020. "Introduction: History of party formation." www.mca.org.my/2/Content/SinglePage?_param1=21-082020-105957-08-202021&_param2=TS (accessed August 20, 2020).

McCargo, Duncan. 2007. "Thaksin and the resurgence of violence in the Thai South." pp 35–68 in *Rethinking Thailand's Southern Violence*, edited by Duncan McCargo. Singapore: NUS Press.

McCargo, Duncan. 2008. *Tearing Apart the Land: Islam and Legitimacy in Southern Thailand*. Ithaca, NY: Cornell University Press.

McCargo, Duncan. 2012. *Mapping National Anxieties: Thailand's Southern Conflict*. Copenhagen: NIAS Press.

McCargo, Duncan and Krisadawan Hongladarom. 2004. "Contesting Isan-ness: Discourses of politics and identity in Northeast Thailand." *Asian Ethnicity* 5(2):219–234.

Mendoza, Mary Anne S. 2021. "When institutions reinforce regional divides: Comparing Christian and Muslim colonial education policies in the Philippines." *Asian Politics & Policy* 13(1): 90–104.

Mietzner, Marcus, and Burhanuddin Muhtadi. 2019. "The mobilisation of intolerance and its trajectories: Indonesian Muslims' views of religious minorities and ethnic Chinese." pp. 155–174 in *Contentious Belonging: The Place of Minorities in Indonesia*, edited by Greg Fealy and Ronit Ricci. Singapore: ISEAS Publishing.

Mohamad, Mahathir. 1970. *The Malay Dilemma*. Singapore: Asia Pacific Press.

Montalvo, Jose G., and Marta Reynal-Querol. 2002. "The effect of ethnic and religious conflict on growth." IVIE WP-EC. www.econ.upf.edu/~ montalvo/wp/rel_ethn.pdf (accessed April 10, 2021).

Morita, Liang. 2007. "Discussing assimilation and language shift among the Chinese in Thailand." *International Journal of the Sociology of Language* 186:43–58.

Mulyanto, Randy. 2019. "'No place like home': Ethnic Chinese who fled Indonesia for Taiwan remember the deadly 1998 riots that changed their lives." *South China Morning Post* (May 14, 2019).

Murdoch, John B. 1974. "The 1901–1902 "Holy Man's" Rebellion." *The Journal of the Siam Society* 62(1):47–66.

Noh, Abdillah. 2014. "Malaysia's dilemma: Economic reforms but politics stay the same." *Southeast Asian Affairs* 2014(1):190–202.

Ockey, James. 2008. "Elections and political integration in the lower south of Thailand." pp 124–154 in *Thai South and Malay North: Ethnic Interactions on a Plural Peninsula*, edited by Michael J. Montesano and Patrick Jory. Singapore: NUS Press.

Ong, Elvin. 2020. "Unequal political representation in the federation of Malaysia: Singapore's entry and exit from 1963–1965." Working Paper.

Ostwald, Kai. 2014. *Engineering identity: The role of the state in shaping ethnic and civic identity in Singapore and Malaysia*. PhD dissertation in Political Science. San Diego: University of California, San Diego.

Ostwald, Kai, and Steven Oliver. 2020. "Four arenas: Malaysia's 2018 election, reform, and democratization." *Democratization* 27(4):662–680.

Ostwald, Kai, Elvin Ong, and Dimitar Gueorguiev. 2019. "Language politics, education, and ethnic integration: The pluralist dilemma in Singapore." *Politics, Groups, and Identities* 7(1):89–108.

Ostwald, Kai, and Mohamed Salihin Subhan. 2021. "Regional identity formation in Malaysia: Primacy of the political center and its essentialized ethnic identities." *Asian Politics and Policy* 13(1): 37–55.

Parks, Thomas I. 2009. "Maintaining peace in a neighborhood torn by separatism: The case of Satun province in Southern Thailand." *Small Wars & Insurgencies* 20(1):185–202.

Pattana Kitiarsa. 2005. "Beyond syncretism: Hybridization of popular religion in contemporary Thailand." *Journal of Southeast Asian Studies* 36(3):461–487.

Peterson, Daniel. 2020. *Islam, Blasphemy, and Human Rights in Indonesia: The Trial of Ahok*. Abingdon: Routledge.

Pongphisoot Busbarat. 2016. "Family making in Sino-Thai Relations." *Kyoto Review of Southeast Asia* 18.

Pongsakorn Wangkumhang, Philip James Shaw, Kridsadakorn Chaichompu, et al. 2013. "Insight into the peopling of mainland Southeast Asia from Thai population genetic structure." *PLoS ONE* 8(11):e79522.

Posner, Daniel N. 2004. "Measuring ethnic fractionalization in Africa." *American Journal of Political Science* 48(4):849–863.

Posner, Daniel N. 2005. *Institutions and Ethnic Politics in Africa*. New York: Cambridge University Press.

Prasad, Karolina. 2016. *Identity Politics and Elections in Malaysia and Indonesia*. Abingdon: Routledge.

Presiden Republik Indonesia. 1998. "Instruksi Presiden Republik Indonesia Nomor 26 Tahun 1998 Tentang Menghentikan Penggunaan Istilah Preibumi dan Non Preibumi" [Instruction of the President of Republic of Indonesia. Number 26 Year 1998. Ending the Use of Pribumi and Non-Pribumi Terms]. Issued September 16, 1998. www.bphn.go.id/data/docu ments/98ip026.pdf (accessed November 6, 2021).

Presiden Republik Indonesia. 1999. "Instruksi Presiden Republik Indonesia Nomor 4 Tahun 1999" [Presidential Instruction of the Republic of Indonesia Number 4 of Year 1999.] Issued May 5, 1999. www.bphn.go.id/data/docu ments/99ip004.pdf (accessed August 26, 2020).

Presiden Republik Indonesia. 2002. "Keputusan Presiden Republik Indonesia Nomor 19 Tahun 2002 Tentang Tahun Baru Imlek" [Presidential Decree of the Republic of Indonesia Number 19 Year 2002 Concerning Chinese New Year.] Issued April 9, 2002. https://peraturan.bpk.go.id/Home/Details/56514/ keppres-no-19-tahun-2002 (accessed August 26, 2020).

Presiden Republik Indonesia. 2014. "Keputusan Presiden Republik Indonesia Nomor 12 Tahun 2014 Tentang Pencabutan Suat Edaran Presidium Kabinet Ampera Nomor SE-06/Pres.Kab/6/1967, Tanggal 28 Juni 1967" [Presidential Decree of the Republic of Indonesia Number 12 of Year 2014 Concerning the Revocation of a Circular of the Presidium of the Ampera Cabinet Number SE-06/Pres.Kab/6/1967, dated 28 June 1967. Issued March 12, 2014. https:// peraturan.bpk.go.id/Home/Details/57561/keppres-no-12-tahun-2014 (accessed August 26, 2020).

Purdey, Jemma. 2006a. *Anti-Chinese Violence in Indonesia, 1996–1999*. Singapore: NUS Press.

Purdey, Jemma. 2006b. "The" other" May riots: Anti-Chinese violence in Solo, May 1998." pp. 72–89 in *Violent Conflicts in Indonesia: Analysis, Representation, Resolution*, edited by Charles A Coppel. Abingdon: Taylor and Francis.

Rahim, Lily Zubaidah. 1998. *The Singapore Dilemma: The Political and Educational Marginality of the Malay Community*. Oxford: Oxford University Press.

Rahim, Lily Zubaidah. 2008. "Winning and losing Malay support: PAP-Malay community relations, 1950s-1960s." pp. 95–115 in *Paths Not Taken: Political Pluralism in Post-War Singapore*, edited by Michael D. Barr and Carl A. Trockie. Singapore: NUS Press.

Rahman Putra al-Haj, Abdul. 1978. *Viewpoints*. Kuala Lumpur: Heinemann Educational Books Ltd.

Rakhmat, Muhammad Zulfikar. 2020 (August 4). "Indonesia must tackle corona-driven growth in anti-Chinese xenophobia." *Nikkei Asia*. https://asia.nikkei.com/Opinion/Indonesia-must-tackle-corona-driven-growth-in-anti-Chinese-xenophobia.

Reynolds, Craig J. 1973. *The Buddhist monkhood in nineteenth century Thailand*. PhD dissertation in History. Ithaca, NY: Cornell University.

Ricks, Jacob I. 2019. "Proud to be Thai: The puzzling absence of ethnicity-based political cleavages in Northeastern Thailand." *Pacific Affairs* 92(2):257–285.

Ricks, Jacob I. 2020. "The effect of language on political appeal: Results from a survey experiment in Thailand." *Political Behavior* 2020(42):83–104.

Ricks, Jacob I. 2021. "The power of state nationalism: Lao ethnics and the Thai identity." Working Paper. Singapore Management University.

Rodan, Garry. 2018. "Singapore's elected president: A failed institution." *Australian Journal of International Affairs* 72:10–15.

Roosa, John. 2006. *Pretext for Mass Murder: The September 30th Movement and Suharto's Coup d'etat in Indonesia*. Madison: University of Wisconsin Press.

Santoso, Joko. 2016. "Sustaining anti-Chinese sentiment in Jakarta." *New Mandala* (March 18, 2016).

Saowanee Alexander. 2021. "Sticky rice in the blood: Isan people's involvement in Thailand's 2020 anti-government protests." *Critical Asian Studies* DOI: 10.1080/14672715.2021.1882867.

Saowanee T. Alexander, and Duncan McCargo. 2014. "Diglossia and identity in Northeast Thailand: Linguistic, social, and political hierarchy." *Journal of Sociolinguistics* 18(1):60–86.

Saowanee T. Alexander, and Duncan McCargo. 2019. "Exit, voice, (dis)loyalty? Northeast Thailand after the 2014 Coup." pp 90–113 in *After the Coup:*

The National Council for Peace and Order Era and the Future of Thailand. Singapore: ISEAS Publishing.

Schulze, Kirsten E. 2017. "The 'ethnic' in Indonesia's communal conflicts: Violence in Ambon, Poso, and Sambas." *Ethnic and Racial Studies* 40(12):2096–2114.

Selway, Joel. 2007. "Turning Malays into Thai-men: Nationalism, ethnicity and economic inequality in Thailand." *South East Asia Research* 15(1):53–87.

Selway, Joel Sawat. 2011. "The measurement of cross-cutting cleavages and other multidimensional cleavage structures." *Political Analysis* 19(1):48–65.

Selway, Joel Sawat. 2015. *Coalitions of the Well-Being: How Electoral Rules and Ethnic Politics Shape Health Policy in Developing Countries.* New York: Cambridge University Press.

Selway, Joel Sawat. 2020. "Thai national identity and Lanna identity in Northern Thailand." *Kyoto Review of Southeast Asia* 27.

Selway, Joel Sawat. 2021. "The Shinawatra siblings: Ethnic heroes and the rise of Lanna nationalism." *Asian Politics and Policy* 13(1): 105–127.

Setijadi, Charlotte. 2015. "Being Chinese again: Learning Mandarin in post-Suharto Indonesia." pp. 141–160 in *Multilingualism in the Chinese Diaspora Worldwide: Transnational Connections and Local Social Realities*, edited by Wei Li. New York: Routledge.

Setijadi, Charlotte. 2017a. "Chinese Indonesians in the eyes of the pribumi public." *ISEAS Perspective* 73(2017).

Setijadi, Charlotte. 2017b. "The Jakarta election continues: What next for embattled Governor Ahok?" *ISEAS Perspective* 18(2017).

Setijadi, Charlotte. 2019. "Anti-Chinese sentiment and the 'return'of the pribumi discourse." pp. 194–213 in *Contentious Belonging: The Place of Minorities in Indonesia*, edited by Greg Fealy and Ronit Ricci. Singapore: ISEAS Publishing.

Siegel, James T. 1998. "Early thoughts on the violence of May 13 and 14, 1998 in Jakarta." *Indonesia* (66):75–108.

Skinner, G. Williams. 1950. "Report on the Chinese in Southeast Asia." Report for Department of Far Eastern Studies. Ithaca, NY: Cornell University.

Skinner, G. Williams. 1957. *Chinese Society in Thailand: An Analytical History.* Ithaca, NY: Cornell University Press.

Skinner, G. Williams. 1958. "The Chinese of Java." pp. 1–10 in *Colloquium on Overseas Chinese*, edited by Morton H. Fried. New York: Institute of Pacific Relations.

Skinner, G. Williams. 1960. "Change and persistence in Chinese culture overseas: A comparison of Thailand and Java." *Journal of the South Seas Society* 16:86–100.

Skinner, G. Williams. 1963. "The Chinese Minority." pp. 97–117 in *Indonesia*, edited by Ruth T. McVey. New Haven, CT: HRAF Press.

Slater, Dan. 2003. "Iron cage in an iron fist: Authoritarian institutions and the personalization of power in Malaysia." *Comparative Politics* 36(1):81–101.

Slater, Dan, and Daniel Ziblatt. 2013. "The enduring indispensability of the controlled comparison." *Comparative Political Studies* 46(10):1301–1127.

Smalley, William A. 1994. *Linguistic Diversity and National Unity: Language Ecology in Thailand*. Chicago, IL: University of Chicago Press.

Soedirgo, Jessica. 2020. *The threat of small things: Patterns of repression and mobilization against micro-sized groups in Indonesia*. PhD dissertation in Political Science. Toronto: University of Toronto.

Soeharto. 1991. *My Thoughts, Words and Deeds: An Autobiography*. Jakarta: Pt. Citra Lamtoro Gung Persada.

Somchai Phatharathananunth. 2002. "Political resistance in Isan." *Tai Culture* 7(1):106–132.

Sophorntavy, Vorng. 2017. *A Meeting of Masks: Status, Power, and Hierarchy in Bangkok*. Copenhagen: NIAS press.

Sterkens, Carl, Agnes Zenaida Camacho, and Peer Scheepers. 2016. "Ethno-religious identification and latent conflict: Support of violence among Muslim and Christian Filipino children and youth." *Conflict, Violence and Peace*: 1–16.

Stimpfl, Joseph. 2006. "Growing up Malay in Singapore." pp. 61–93 in *Race, Ethnicity, and the State in Malaysia and Singapore*, edited by Kwen Fee Lian. Leiden: Brill.

Strate, Shane. 2015. *The Lost Territories: Thailand's History of National Humiliation*. Honolulu: University of Hawaii Press.

Strauch, Judith. 1981. "Chinese new villages of the Malayan emergency, a generation later: A case study." *Contemporary Southeast Asia* 3(2):126–139.

Streckfuss, David. 1993. "The mixed colonial legacy in Siam: Origins of Thai racialist thought, 1890–1910." pp. 123–153 in *Autonomous Histories, Particular Truths: Essay in Honor of John R.W. Smail*, edited by Laurie J. Sears and John Smail. Madison: University of Wisconsin Center for Southeast Asian Studies.

Streckfuss, David. 2015. "An 'ethnic' reading of 'Thai' history in the twilight of the century-old official 'Thai' national model." *South East Asia Research* 20(3):305–327.

Streicher, Ruth. 2020. *Uneasy Military Encounters: The Imperial Politics of Counterinsurgency in Southern Thailand*. Ithica, NY: Cornell University Press.

Suhrke, Astri. 1977. "Loyalists and separatists: The Muslims in Southern Thailand." *Asian Survey* 17(3):237–250.

Sukma, Rizal. 2003. *Indonesia and China: The Politics of a Troubled Relationship*. London: Routledge.

Sumaktoyo, Nathaneal. 2021. "Ethnic and religious sentiments in Indonesian politics: Evidence from the 2017 Jakarta Gubernatorial Election." *Journal of East Asian Studies* 21(1):1–24. doi: 10.1017/jea.2020.35.

Supreme Court Singapore. 2020. www.supremecourt.gov.sg/ (accessed August 21, 2020).

The Sunday Times. 1959a. "Institute of Malayan Culture." (August 23).

The Sunday Times. 1959b. "Translating done free during L-Week." (March 25).

The Sunday Times. 1966. "Ong: There's no language issue." (November 22).

Suryadinata, Leo. 1976. "Indonesian policies toward the Chinese minority under the new order." *Asian Survey* 16(8):770–787.

Suryadinata, Leo (ed.). 1997. *Ethnic Chinese as Southeast Asians*. Singapore: ISEAS Press.

Suryadinata, Leo. 2005. "Buddhism and Confucianism in contemporary Indonesia: Recent developments." pp. 77–94 in *Chinese Indonesians: Remembering, Distorting, Forgetting*, edited by Tim Lindsey and Helen Pausacker. Singapore: ISEAS Publications.

Suryadinata, Leo. 2008. "Chinese Indonesians in an era of globalization: Some major characteristics." pp. 1–16 in *Ethnic Chinese in Contemporary Indonesia*, edited by Leo Suryadinata. Singapore: Chinese Heritage Centre and ISEAS.

Suryadinata, Leo. 2019. "Chinese participation in the 2019 Indonesian election." *ISEAS Perspective* 58(2019).

Susilo, Daniel, and Rahma Sugihartati. 2020. "Indonesian nationalism discourse on YouTube video produced by young Chinese-Indonesians." *Plaridel* Advance Online Publication. https://doi.org/10.52518/2020-02rahma.

Suwilai Premsrirat, Suchritlaks Dipdung, Aekphong Suwankesd, et al. 2004. *Phaenthi Phasa khong Klumchatphan Tang-tang nai Prathed Thai* [Ethnolinguistic maps of Thailand]. Bangkok: Mahidol University.

Tajima, Yuhki. 2014. *The Institutional Origins of Communal Violence: Indonesia's Transition from Authoritarian Rule*. New York: Cambridge University Press.

Tajima, Yuhki, Krislert Samphantharak, and Kai Ostwald. 2018. "Ethnic segregation and public goods: Evidence from Indonesia." *American Political Science Review*: 1–17.

Tan, Eugene K. B. 2005. "Multiracialism engineered: The limits of electoral and spatial integration in Singapore." *Ethnopolitics* 4(4):413–428.

Tan, Eugene K. B. 2007. "The multilingual state in search of the nation: The language policy and discourse in Singapore's nation-building." pp. 74–117 in *Language, Nation and Development in Southeast Asia*, edited by Hock Guan Lee and Leo Suryadinata. Singapore: ISEAS.

Tan, Kenneth Paul. 2018. *Singapore: Identity, Brand, Power*. New York: Cambridge University Press.

Tan, Mely G. 2004. "Unity in diversity: Ethnic Chinese and nation-building in Indonesia." pp. 20–44 in *Ethnic Relations and Nation-Building in Southeast Asia: The Case of the Ethnic Chinese*, edited by Leo Suryadinata. Singapore: Singapore Society of Asian Studies and ISEAS.

Tan, Siok Sun. 2007. *Goh Keng Swee: A Portrait*. Singapore: Editions Didier Millet.

Tang, Chaoju. 2009. *Mutual Intelligibility of Chinese Dialects: An Experimental Approach*. Utrech: LOT.

Tarling, Nicholas. 2004. *Nationalism in Southeast Asia*. London: Routledge Curzon.

Thanet Aphornsuvan. 2008. "Origins of Malay Muslim "separatism" in Southern Thailand." pp 91–123 in *Thai South and Malay North: Ethnic Interactions on a Plural Peninsula*, edited by Michael J. Montesano and Patrick Jory. Singapore: NUS Press.

Thongchai Winichakul. 1994. *Siam Mapped: A History of the Geo-body of a Nation*. Honolulu: University of Hawaii Press.

Toha, Risa J. 2017. "Political competition and ethnic riots in democratic transition: A lesson from indonesia." *British Journal of Political Science* 47(3):631–651.

Ukrist Pathmanand. 2006. "Thaksin's Achilles' heel: The failure of hawkish approaches in the Thai south." *Critical Asian Studies* 38(01):73–93.

van der Kroef, Justus M. 1976. "Race and class in Indonesia: Patterns of discrimination and conflict." pp 213 in *Case Studies on Human Rights and Fundamental Freedoms: A World Survey*, edited by Willem A. Veenhoven. The Hague: Nijhoff.

Van Roy, Edward. 2016. "Contending identities: Islam and ethnicity in Old Bangkok." *Journal of the Siam Society* 104:169–202.

Varshney, Ashutosh, Zulfan Tadjoeddin, and Rizal Panggabean. 2010. "Patterns of collective violence in Indonesia." *Collective Violence in Indonesia*:19–49.

Velayutham, Selvaraj. 2017. "Races without racism?: Everyday race relations in Singapore." *Identities* 24(4):455–473.

Vella, Walter F. 1978. *Chaiyo! King Vajiravudh and the Development of Thai Nationalism*. Honolulu: University of Hawai'i Press.

Vickery, Michael. 1970. "Thai regional elites and the reforms of King Chulalongkorn." *Journal of Asian Studies* 29(4):863–881.

Voltaire. 2017. "Inderjit Singh: A sitting MP resigning from office to contest Presidential Election may go against spirit of Office as intended by Lee Kuan Yew." *The Independent* (July 28, 2017).

Wan Kadir Che Man. 1987. *Muslim separatism: The Moros in Southern Philippines and the Malays in Southern Thailand*. PhD dissertation. Australia National University.

Wang, Gungwu. 2002. "Islam versus Asia's Chinese diaspora." *Project Syndicate*, July 29, 2002. www.project-syndicate.org/commentary/islam-versus-asia-s-chinese-diaspora (accessed November 6, 2021).

Wang, Gungwu. 2004. "Chinese ethnicity in New Southeast Asian nations." pp 1–19 in *Ethnic Relations and Nation-Building in Southeast Asia*, edited by Leo Suryadinata. Singapore: ISEAS Publishing.

Ware, Anthony, and Costas Laoutides. 2018. *Myanmar's 'Rohingya' Conflict*. New York: Oxford University Press.

Wasana Wongsurawat. 2019. *The Crown and the Capitalists: The Ethnic Chinese and the Founding of the Thai Nation*. Seattle: University of Washington Press.

Wibhu Kutanan, Thitika Kitpipit, Sukanya Phetpeng, and Phuvadol Thanakiatkrai. 2014. "Forensic STR loci reveal common genetic ancestry of the Thai-Malay Muslims and Thai Buddhists in the deep southern region of Thailand." *Journal of Human Genetics* 59:675–681.

Wijayanta, Hanibal W. Y. 1998. "Percik Bara Seantero Nusantara" [A Smoldering Stain Throughout the Archipelago]. Jakarta: Forum Keadilan (June 1, 1998):18–22.

Wimmer, Andreas. 2013. *Ethnic Boundary Making: Institutions, Power, Networks*. New York: Oxford University Press.

Winarta, Frans H. 2008. "No more discrimination against the Chinese." pp. 57–74 in *Ethnic Chinese in Contemporary Indonesia*, edited by Leo Suryadinata. Singapore: Chinese Heritage Centre and ISEAS.

Winyu Ardrugsa. 2014. "Bangkok Muslims: Social otherness and territorial conceptions." Paper presented at the 12th International Conference on Thai Studies. April 22–24. University of Sydney.

Wu, Chun-Ying. 2021. *How political regimes shape minority language education: Evidence from Southeast Asia and Taiwan*. PhD dissertation in Government. Austin: University of Texas.

Wyatt, David K. 1966. *The beginnings of modern education in Thailand: 1868–1910*. PhD dissertation in History. Ithaca, NY: Cornell University.

Wyatt, David K. 2003. Thailand: A Short History. New Haven, CT: Yale University Press.

Yahuda, Michael B. 2004. *The International Politics of the Asia-Pacific.* London: Routledge.

Yong, Ching Fatt, and R. B. McKenna. 1990. *The Kuomintang Movement in British Malaya, 1912–1949.* Singapore: Singapore University Press.

Acknowledgments

This Element benefited tremendously from Singapore Management University's Short-Term Research Collaboration Program, which allowed us to work together in Singapore for a week in January 2020 just before COVID-19 ravaged the world. Jake also enjoyed a Lee Kong Chian Fellowship that supported the writing of the piece. We express our gratitude to Sebastian Dettman, Dean Dulay, Colm Fox, Jangai Jap, and Charlotte Setijadi for feedback. We also want to thank the three anonymous reviewers: They provided extensive comments that strengthened our argument and discussion of the cases – truly above and beyond the call of duty. Furthermore, the editorial staff at Cambridge deserves mention for their alacrity. And finally, many thanks to Ed Aspinall and Meredith Weiss for their comments, support, and accommodation throughout this process. We, of course, are responsible for any mistakes.

Cambridge Elements ≡

Politics and Society in Southeast Asia

Edward Aspinall

Australian National University

Edward Aspinall is a professor of politics at the Coral Bell School of Asia-Pacific Affairs, Australian National University. A specialist of Southeast Asia, especially Indonesia, much of his research has focused on democratisation, ethnic politics and civil society in Indonesia and, most recently, clientelism across Southeast Asia.

Meredith L. Weiss

University at Albany, SUNY

Meredith L. Weiss is Professor of Political Science at the University at Albany, SUNY. Her research addresses political mobilization and contention, the politics of identity and development, and electoral politics in Southeast Asia, with particular focus on Malaysia and Singapore.

About the Series

The Elements series Politics and Society in Southeast Asia includes both country-specific and thematic studies on one of the world's most dynamic regions. Each title, written by a leading scholar of that country or theme, combines a succinct, comprehensive, up-to-date overview of debates in the scholarly literature with original analysis and a clear argument.

Cambridge Elements ≡

Politics and Society in Southeast Asia

Elements in the Series

A full series listing is available at: www.cambridge.org/ESEA